To Whom It May Concern

To Whom It May Concern

By

MARVIN O. ASHTON

BOOKCRAFT PUBLISHING CO.
SALT LAKE CITY, UTAH
1951

FOURTH EDITION

PRINTED IN THE UNITED STATES OF AMERICA
BY
SUN LITHO. CO.
SALT LAKE CITY, UTAH - U. S. A.

Contents

CONTENTS

CONTENTS—*Continued*

PUBLISHER'S NOTE:—Bishop Marvin O. Ashton died suddenly during the early morning of October 7, 1946, a few short weeks after completing this manuscript and making final preparations for its publication. This book, altered only to include his portrait and a short biographical sketch, will stand as a monument to his lifetime of service in the Church of Jesus Christ of Latter-day Saints.

MARVIN O. ASHTON

Marvin Owen Ashton came into the world by the light of a kerosene lamp late at night during an April shower. He was born April 8, 1883, in a red brick house his father had built in Salt Lake City, Utah.

His father, Edward T. Ashton, was a pioneer builder. His mother, Effie Morris Ashton, was the daughter of another prominent Mormon builder, Elias Morris, from Wales.

From his childhood days when he had long golden ringlets and wore pleated skirts, people liked Marvin Ashton. And he loved them. As a boy he would slip through the hole in the Ashton board fence to run errands for his father's aunt, a widow. He championed a meek and often-ragged neighbor boy who had peculiar eyes and a twisted mouth.

His father's yard was a gathering place for boys. Marvin tricked with them on the horizontal bar, which was a discarded pipe or shovel handle between two posts. From his mother's old stockings he knitted baseballs, and he promoted wrestling tournaments in his father's barn. He was an ace at marbles, but often returned his winnings to the loser. He splashed in the Jordan River in the summer and skated on a near-by canal in the winter. He led the torchlight processions of neighborhood boys with lighted rags on a broomstick in one hand and a whirling stick on the finger of the other.

In grade school, Marvin Ashton excelled in the spelling bees and debating matches. Later, at L. D. S. College he was manager of the school paper and president of his class.

Some of the first money he earned came from his boyhood rabbitry. A tin can high on a cupboard shelf received a tenth of his earnings for tithing. He later worked for his father by driving a horse-drawn two wheel cart loaded with building materials. A tall, big-framed young man with curly hair (which he would wet down hard "so I won't look like a sissy"), he laid bricks and later taught school, eight grades in one little building in rural Coonville near Salt Lake City. After that he was a school principal at neighboring Pleasant Green.

Following his marriage in the Salt Lake Temple to Rae Jeremy in 1906 and his mission to Great Britain two years later, he climbed fast in the business world. He became manager of a lumber company and later a founder and first manager of another, which he developed into one of the largest retail building supply houses in the intermountain region. He was elected president of Utah Lumber Dealers Association, and first president of the Sugar House Rotary club. He was president of the Sugar House Businessmen's League. Later he represented the Church in several large business enterprises. As a civic leader his achievements are legion. He led out in the erection of a massive pioneer monument in Sugar House, and in the campaign that brought an imposing post office there. He crusaded for the removal of the state prison from residential Salt Lake City. He was a lawmaker in Utah's legislature.

Marvin O. Ashton campaigned for funds for the Salvation Army, because, he explained, "They reach into places we don't get." He advocated adult education, himself enrolling for courses despite heavy Church and business demands. He believed in eternal progression.

In the Church, Marvin O. Ashton moved up from Sunday School superintendent to first bishop of Wasatch ward, to member of Granite stake high council and then into its presidency, to first president of Highland stake and finally to first counselor in the Presiding Bishopric. As a member of the Granite stake presidency, he organized a welfare program that fed hundreds of hungry mouths. A beautiful new meetinghouse was erected while he was ward bishop. A splendrous stake house was reared when he was in the Granite Stake presidency, while he was chairman of the building committee.

He vigorously promoted the Church beautification program during the 1930's and 1940's.

But with all his achievements, Marvin O. Ashton was preeminently a man of the people, a great commoner. As a young man, though his means were modest, he often treated his entire group to drugstore ice cream. Later, he would bundle his family into his yellow-spoked Ford with flapping side curtains, and go visiting widows in need. He did not stop with kind words and baskets of food. He checked the coalbin, the mortgage on the house, the children's clothes, and their education. During the depression of the 1930's, when he himself grubbed hard to sustain his own family of eight, he somehow found enough coins in his purse to feed others. Among them was an old, bent, and wizened widow, not a member of the Church, who lived near-by. He discovered that his birthday anniversary was also hers. He always took her a special gift on that occasion.

"Mother, put some more water in the soup," he would often call to his Rae. Then he would usher in dinner guests—a strange boy he had found on the highway or Indians or truck drivers from the lumberyard or a big businessman from the East.

Bishop Ashton loved youth. He gathered the neighborhood children around his outdoor fireplace. With his big chef's apron, he treated them to hamburgers and entertained them by telling stories and by balancing objects, from brooms to tables, on his chin. He liked to take his sons hunting for wild rabbits.

Once as a young man, while driving his horse and buggy, a boy hurled a snowball at him. It caught him squarely in the face. Leaping from the buggy, he pursued the lad. After a winding chase he caught him. Bringing his big hands down on the boy's shoulders, he looked the small fellow in the eye.

Then he said, "You little rascal—I'd do the same thing if I were you."

High and low sought Bishop Ashton's counsel. A father phoned him long distance nearly one-thousand miles one night for advice on his wayward son. A candidate sought his opinion before accepting the nomination for governor. Mayors, prison wardens, bishops, stake presidents, and all types of people in trouble brought him their problems. Once a police chief phoned him and requested that he gather his family together for a special prayer for the chief's granddaughter who had been struck by an automobile.

"He knew everyone he met," one of Bishop Ashton's friends once said. Untold numbers referred to him as "My best friend."

Courage, integrity, and frankness walked and talked with Marvin O. Ashton. "Let's speak the English language," he would say.

Bishop Ashton made people laugh. His quick wit sparkled around the campfire or the hospital bed or the banquet table (he never once yielded to wearing a tuxedo despite all his formal engagements).

At the last session of the semi-annual general conference of the Church on October 6, 1946, Bishop Ashton spoke in the Salt Lake Tabernacle. He gave one of his usual "down-to-earth" talks in the vivid, homespun language that was so characteristic of him. The night following, he slept away into eternity, a victim of a heart attack in his own home.

Next day one of the General Authorities reasoned: "Who better deserved to pass on in the twinkling of an eye?" Another admirer said: "His was a large body, but it simply wasn't adequate enough to house his big, expanding heart. And so it burst."

INTRODUCTION

It is the writer's judgment that you won't find in this book very much that is new. In fact, he believes you will find it to be rather old-fashioned. The lessons that the author has tried to tell have been told for a thousand years. However, he makes no apology for its being old-fashioned. After all, over the centuries human nature hasn't changed. The model of your car changes almost every year—so does your vacuum cleaner, and, of course, your radio and even your clothes change style. But for some reason this old physique of ours stays pretty much the same. A babe born this morning, even though attended with all the most modern parade of doctors, nurses, and apparatus, has the same chassis and the same motor inside that controlled that wriggling piece of anatomy of a babe born the night the walls of Jericho tumbled over.

A worried modern mother in hysterics because her baby had a cold on its chest, desperately sought the advice of the family physician over the telephone. All excited she nervously said to the doctor. "What shall I do? What shall I do?" Calmly the family health consultant inquired of the mother, "My dear, have you tried a mustard plaster?" Impulsively the child's mother thundered back at the doctor, "But, Doctor, isn't a mustard plaster old-fashioned?" "Yes," answered the physician, "but so is your baby."

Now if a mustard plaster was used one hundred years ago for a cold that threatened to develop into pneumonia, with the same medical logic a child in 1946 should have the flesh around his wishbone reddened with the burning of this thing called mustard. What was good medicine for the human body before the flood is good now. We have the same problems in fighting dishonesty and liquor now as men had in the first history of civilization on the banks of the Nile River.

A story adds color to a lesson and puts the teeth into it. Stories are to a lesson what raisins are to a cookie.

President B. S. Hinckley tells an interesting story about one of his missionaries in the Northern States Mission. The good fellow had been coached somewhat in public speaking, and Brother Hinckley attended a meeting where our preacher of the gospel had a chance to show his virtues along the line suggested. His subject was the Prodigal Son. He did very well. After the meeting the president of the mission complimented him on his speech. Said President Hinckley, "That was a splendid talk, Brother ————, but where did you get the authority to call that fatted calf a 'spotted calf'?" The young man had an answer all ready. Said he to his mission president, "Haven't you always instructed us to add as much *color* to our talks as we could?"

Noise never counts. What counts is hitting the bull's eye of human interest. Everybody likes a story. Lincoln, undoubtedly the greatest teacher that America has produced, taught great fundamentals with stories. Lincoln in speaking once of a "loud" but not "logical" speaker said that this fellow was like a boat which used to travel up and down the Mississippi—the engine was mostly boiler and so constructed in its relation to the whistle that whenever the whistle sent an awfully loud sound for miles about, the boat stopped.

Now in the venture of this book the author must confess he has used many stories. They are stories he has heard since his childhood. Some of them are as old as the hills, and some you have heard or read elsewhere probably many times. Some wise fellow has observed that most of us who use stories, as far as the story business is concerned, are retailers. If as you read these pages, you find a story that you yourself brought into the world for the first time, pardon its repetition. The author is decidedly playing the role of a retailer. You'll admit that a good story, unless it has been used until it's threadbare, is like an old tune that hits your heart. You like to hear it again and again. No claim is made in this book for very much originality. One uses a story one way—the other fellow springs it to clinch another point entirely. The main virtue of a story is in its application.

Now just a word about the cartoons: This book in its appearance, using many cartoons, looks like a spotted hyena. The writer makes no apology for this either. We don't use the cartoonist half as much as we should. After all, the only excuse for the English language is to express thought. What we all like about a cartoon is that it tells a story without boring us. Someone has compared public speaking to drilling for petroleum. He has advised as follows: "When you don't strike oil, stop boring." We remember what we see longer than what we hear. A story in a picture strikes you straight in the eye, and if it is done accurately and well, it breaks right through mentality and *rings the bell.* And it goes without saying that if a cartoonist sells his wares, he's got to have a good supply of this thing we call "*humor.*" Humor overdone will go as flat as a pancake. If it is wholesome and clean, even in Church, with propriety, it has a tremendous wallop in moral teaching.

I want to take my hat off here to J. A. Bywater and Nelson White who are responsible for most of the illustrations in this book. They are real artists, and if this humble book has any merit at all, the author wants them to get a decided good portion of credit. I thank them for their wonderful cooperation.

A glance at the subjects discussed herein tells the observer that this book is a combination of "*pot shots.*" They are shots taken almost at random. While some items interest some folks more than others, all in all the writer believes there is nothing here in the general philosophy of things that might not be good for everyone who pretends to be a good Latter-day Saint or a good citizen in general. Some pages are directed to bishops, but the observations could consistently apply to most executives or leaders on our wards and stakes, or for that matter, to any group leader whatsoever.

For the last two years the author has written a few articles for *The Improvement Era.* While they were humbly written, they called forth a comment or two which made the writer feel that maybe they were causing some interest. Many suggested he put these into a book. He has added other little chapters, and this book is dedicated TO WHOM IT MAY CONCERN.

From a literary standpoint this book won't take many yards of blue ribbon. If there is enough common sense and the spirit of human kindness interwoven into the chapters of this book to cause someone to Stop, Look, and Listen in his journey of life, the author shall be most happy. If the by-product of this book may bring to its readers more faith in our Creator and the general scheme of things, the author will feel paid for this humble effort.

—THE AUTHOR.

TO WHOM IT
MAY CONCERN

STORY ONE

TAKE THE MIDDLE ROAD

One of the greatest compliments you can pay a fellow is to tell him he is well-balanced. It is easier to find intellect than it is sound judgment. Very often when you find a mind that can cut some wonderful capers, you also in the same parcel find a brain that is eccentric. The Good Old Book eternally tries to burn it into us, "with all thy learning get understanding." One of the saddest pictures in this world of ours is a fellow brimming over with brain fervor but not balanced.

When we say our prayers at night, it might be very appropriate for us all to plead very *vehemently* to the heavens above, "Lord, bless me with common sense." Another name for this latter word is "gumption." Some call it "horse sense." If we meant business when we prayed for blessings, we would have fewer one-track minds. As a fellow observed, "Yes, and some of them are mighty narrow gauged at that."

In our traveling through life too many of us are like a horse that isn't bridle wise. We go headlong to the left or headlong to the right. Let's keep the middle of the road. There is a bar pit on either side. One is humiliation and embarrassment, and the other downright ruin. Our artist here has done a real job in putting the picture before us. *Take the middle road.*

In plain American English, are you so terribly practical that you see only the dollar sign and worship it to the extent of being blind to worth-while values? In other words, are you money crazy? "He who longs to be rich is like a man who drinks

Take The Middle Road
THE MIDDLE ROAD
POVERTY
BAD
DEBTS
ETC.
HAPPINESS
DISAPPOINTMENT
AND
DISILLUSIONMENT

sea water. The more he drinks the more thirsty he becomes and never leaves off until he perishes." (I wish I knew who gave us those lines of inspiration. I would like to take my hat off to him.)

I remember a story in the scriptures. It was an observation of the Christ. A certain man built huge barns and jammed the barns with grain and the necessities of life. He had enough to last for years. He shut himself from the world and sat down and chuckled to himself that he had so much. I think that it was then that God said this unto him: "Thou fool, this night thy soul shall be required of thee." (Luke 12:20)

The observation I would like to make here is that many people holding positions in our Church are getting this money bug. I take my hat off to the man who has insurance and provides for a rainy day. A man is a coward if he doesn't do that. I am talking about the man who has accumulated plenty and gets the disease or the bug so that he eternally chases after more, more, more, and in that chasing neglects his duties. Some men take the cream of their energy for making money, and when they come to the Lord's work, they've got nothing but skim milk, and some of it is awfully blue. Some organizations succeed in spite of the men at the heads, in spite of what they do and don't do. Some men want the titles, the honor, but like the old darky fishing, they go to sleep holding the line.

Now when you go, you will leave everything. Some men get their minds so much on cattle, so much on stocks and bonds, so much on sheep that they crowd everything else out. Some of our leaders in our organizations get that disease. I once heard of a fellow who got so in love with sheep that he just kept grabbing, grabbing, grabbing, and finally a bishop's court was held to settle to whom a certain herd of sheep belonged. And the court decided against him. When the trial ended, he shook his fist and said: "Well, you've got the sheep, but I'll have those sheep in the next world." Well, now, I don't know too much about those things, but I'll bet that if he has those sheep in the next world he'll have to put some asbestos blankets on them so they will stand the heat.

Some people get this grabbing habit so intensified in their systems that it becomes second nature for them to grab, grab, grab. It so permeates their beings that it works with them like reflex action.

How happy all of us are in each general conference as we are reminded of the sound condition of our Church. I am thinking of the spiritual as well as of the temporal.

When this Church thinks of nothing but money, it is a "goner." When this Church thinks of only spiritual things, and we haven't our feet on the ground, and we won't hold water financially, we are on dangerous ground. Thank the Lord for that balanced condition of this Church, and may it always be that way.

What is true of the Church is true of an individual. Are you balanced? Am I balanced? The man that thinks of nothing but the hereafter and stumbles over the practical things of life is really a picture. It is sad. I am not talking about the man that has his troubles financially—I am talking about the man who eternally has his head in the clouds and never watches his feet below. That fellow, in an exaggerated case, is a leech. He is like the cuckoo bird that lays its eggs in another bird's nest. Yes, others have to hatch the eggs and raise these additional children. What "gumption" this impractical fellow lacks has to be furnished by someone else.

You know there has been nothing so interesting to me as this thing they call mistletoe. Mistletoe is found largely in

Texas, New Mexico, and Arizona. I guess it's found in other places, too. But you see some trees festooned with the mistletoe; that mistletoe is a leech. I don't know why they ever connected the mistletoe with affection, because every time that mistletoe gives that tree a kiss, if enough mistletoes do the same, the tree is a "goner." Yes, in using mistletoe language you can kiss the tree good-bye. And that is going to be the trouble with our nation if we are not very careful. I saw some trees down in Texas that were just a mass of mistletoe. A tree so burdened is going to get the ten count. A man that is not practically balanced is like the mistletoe; he is like the cuckoo bird. A man, on the other hand, who thinks of nothing but money, money, money, is also a "goner."

Don't worry too much if financially the Church is loading you a trifle heavy. Yes, you're paying your fast offering, your tithing, donations to the building fund, ward maintenance, etc., but maybe your being loaded will save you. It will do you good. That is what the world needs. You will always find those people that will come up to you and sympathize with you, as well as a lot of people who do nothing themselves but go around with a chip on their shoulder. Someone has said: "You can bet your life when someone goes around with a chip on his shoulder, there is more wood farther up."

I want to come back to this thought again; the thing that counts in this world is happiness and the contemplating of events over the horizon. Let us be kind to one another and think of something besides money and ambition. That is the trouble with the world.

Ike Eisenhower, our beloved general, was giving a talk to the navy boys one day, and he made this observation: "Cultivate mutual understanding of anyone you have to get along with."

Some good writer commenting on it—I wish I could recall his name so I could give him credit—told this little parable I leave with you. The parable is as follows:

" A newspaper man interviewed a farmer who had won many blue ribbons in raising corn. The newspaper man said: 'I understand you are the winner of some blue ribbons.' 'Yes.' 'But,' he said, 'what gets me is that when you win a blue ribbon, you take your select corn and pass it on to your neighbors, and they are competing against you for the ribbons. What is the sense in it?' The old man replied: "These neighbors all around me have been raising corn, and if I don't give them select corn their bad corn is going to pollinate my good corn."

I read a strange story of a man by the name of Pheister. He experimented in the raising of a hybrid corn. When the corn was in the flower or tassel stage, he tied paper sacks around the tassels so that he could govern the pollinating of it.

You can't do that in life. Your neighbors are there scattering their pollen, as it were, or influence, and so are you—you are living with them. As you help them they help you.

"Give to the world the best you have, and the best will come back to you." (*Life's Mirror.*)

A month ago, going down towards the Mexican line, down where the lizards, as the boy puts it, lie on their backs and fan themselves, we stopped in a little food shop. We didn't get much bodily food, but we did come away with some food for the mind that was hanging on the walls. The one that hit me between the eyes was: "Some people think when they cast their bread upon the water, it should return toasted and buttered."

Now, wait a minute! You may think that is rather ridiculous. That man who sent his corn, his select corn to his neighbors, was casting bread upon the waters, but he got it back toasted and buttered.

May the Lord help us to be kind. Let us remember what is ahead of us. Let's not look gloomy these days. Let's face our problems. Our grandparents did it. Let's keep our chins to the sun and face whatever is ahead of us. We play our greatest tunes in time of trouble, and the challenger is there. You do your duty; let me do mine; and let's smile—smile if it kills us, and if some people smiled it would kill them.

There are sounds in the air more interesting than the rattle of gold. The important thing is, is your anatomy keyed up to hear them? While attending a stake conference the other day, I heard a story told that went right to my bones.

It happened in one of the noisiest and possibly the most wicked cities of America. Two men were walking down one of the clamorous streets of this Babel City. There was the clanking of iron trains overhead, tooting of cars on the surface, and excitement, bustling, and all the trimmings. One of these men was from the country a hundred miles out of the turmoil of this center, the other from the city itself. As they marched along this busy thoroughfare, the farmer stopped the busy city friend and observed, "Did you hear that cricket?" "No, neither did you," came the answer. "Come on back here, and I'll show you," answered his friend.

They walked back a few steps until they came to a little flower shop. They stepped back to the flowers, and on the floor by the side of a pot they found the black insect rubbing his legs together sending to the world its message of good cheer.

After proving his point our rural friend went on to his friend: "In this city you can't hear the sound of the cricket.

Let me show you what sound you can hear." He put his hand in his pocket, drew out a half dollar, and threw it on the pavement. In less time than you can tell it, forty people were struggling to grab on to the silver piece. They did everything but tear out each other's hair. The farmer observed, "That's the sound that doesn't escape your ears."

Yes, that's the trouble in America. As we travel on life's highway, let's tune in on the voice of the cricket. Let's hear the sound of the silver only to the extent that that silver will bring us contentment and happiness. Let's be well-balanced.

"Say your prayers," as Brigham Young advised, " but keep your powder dry."

Take the middle road.

STORY TWO

Let's be tolerant

"They first fell on their knees and then fell on the necks of those who did not believe as they." Chapter I was enacted in 1620. Chapter II was staged just fifty years later.

Sometimes if we are not careful, if we do not ventilate our thinking, zeal turns to tyranny, and then we're in bad shape. This is what happened to our Pilgrim Fathers whose names we so much revere. The other day I took down my old American history books and glanced at some of the illustrated pages.. Only a few years after the landing at Plymouth Rock you find these same people persecuting the poor Quakers. Look at the picture with me—see these "devout" people throwing eggs at these poor Quakers and jeering at them as they rest like tied chickens in the stocks in the public square.

Now let's turn over the pages of this illustrated history book. Now you come to a scene very much like the chapter depicted as our artist is showing us. See that old woman's agony as she marches off at the hands of her religious persecutors.

A couple of years ago President William H. Reeder of the New England States Mission took me over to that famous old wood structure, the House of Seven Gables. A little girl escorted me through the house. She showed me the old fireplace some three hundred years old, including the old style baking facilities. I won't go into detail here, but let me tell you of a little dark spot into which she ushered me. She, as it were, pushed me in and then said, "Now start climbing." She went upstairs another way, and I was left in the dark dungeon. The only way I could move was up. I wished at the time that I had been more careful about my dieting—my avoirdupois bothered me. However, in some way I made it—got to the top. She came forward, and as I came through the miniature door she closed it after me, and all I could see were panels around the room. She put her little fingers in the fireplace and pushed a secret button, and the door at the head of this corkscrew stairway up which I came, sprang open, exposing the secret hole in the wall. She said to me, "This is the stairway that the old women used to hide in during the days of the Salem witchcraft, lest they be hanged."

By the way, I saw the hill where twenty old ladies were hanged because of the tyranny of those religious Pilgrims. I I think the name "Salem" means peace, but it's a good thing those old ladies didn't name the town. They would have called it by some other than a name meaning peace. You remember those dark days—days that are really a stain on American history. The saying goes they used to throw one of those aged ladies in a lake. If she was innocent, she sank; if she was guilty, she floated. I am not sure now whether it was because our Pilgrim fathers stayed too long in Holland that they brought this tyranny over with them or whether they didn't long enough to rid themselves of this iniquity. We are sometimes inclined, if we get a little authority, to crack the whip and forget what real Christianity is.

This piece of history should be a warning and a lesson to all of us. Bigotry and intolerance have made more scorched earth than all the fires in history. "God bless me and my wife, our son John and his wife; us four and no more." That philosophy has caused a good portion of the wars in history.

Is your conception of your Creator something like this?

> Oh, Thou, wha in the Heavens dost dwell
> Wha as it pleases best thysel'
> Sends one to heaven and ten to hell
> a' for they glory,
> And no for any guid or ill
> They've done afore thee!

In ridicule of the "hypocrites" in the ministry of his time in his land Bobbie Burns gave us the above lines.

Charles W. Penrose, president of the British Mission, told a story to us missionaries that I hope will stay with me all my life. Some fellow, according to Brother Penrose, had a peculiar dream and with a definite satire in mind recited it to some overzealous Saints. He said he died and naturally, after getting his bearings, applied at the Pearly Gates for admission. As he approached St. Peter, the latter with his fingers to his lips beckoned the candidate to enter just as noiselessly as possible. As he approached closer the keeper of the gates whispered to him, "Be just as quiet as you can; the Mormons are in the next room. They think they're the only people in heaven, and we don't want to disturb them."

Now I've got too much sense to ridicule our position in the world and the sanctity, if you please, of the restoration of the gospel and the need of same in this upset world. What I am trying to do is to shoot a straight shaft at the heart of bigotry and self-righteousness. We are all God's people or we wouldn't be here. Let's not be happy in any program but one that contemplates the salvation of all mankind. That's the gospel of Jesus Christ.

If we'll be tolerant with those who differ honestly with us, the time will come when we'll be mighty happy we made allowances. If we'd only look at the virtues of others and not everlastingly magnify our differences, we'd be much happier. If another sect differs with us, let us not get all wrought up. The most sacred blessing any of us enjoy is our free agency. Take that away from us, our right to choose what path we will take, then we're nothing more than slaves or dumb cattle.

When we say our prayers at night, it would be a very good thing if we'd ask the Lord to help us see ourselves as others see us.

Father Kelly and Rabbi Levi were chatting together. Said Father Kelly to his Jewish friend, "When are you going to become liberal enough to eat ham with me?" Rabbi Levi answered Father Kelly, "At your wedding."

Sometimes some of us in our anxiety to be zealous really go to town going after the little faults of others. Yes, we forget the beam that is in our own eye and go after field mice in others with a double-barrelled elephant gun. Some of us with faults of elephant magnitude go hunting for field mice weaknesses in others. And besides lacking a sympathy that Christ spent most of his time trying to teach us, "we strain at a gnat and swallow a camel."

Sometimes I have quite a time making myself clear. Let me illustrate: It happened in London when the Germans were dropping blockbusters from the sky. One of those bombs would really transform a whole business block into shreaded wheat. Once in a while a bomb, if it were operated upon immediately after it landed. could be stopped from doing its terrible job. There were soldiers stationed about the bombing zone whose duty it was to tackle immediately the missile from the heavens that hadn't exploded, break off the connections between the clock ticker and the business part of the explosive, and save millions of dollars of property and maybe hundreds of lives. Well, one of these demons from the air lit in a basement. It lay there sizzling, getting ready to play its havoc. The bomb was observed, and an orderly was rushed to it. But the poor fellow, failing to do his duty, jumped up the ladder as white as a ghost. The officer in charge thundered out at the retreating fellow, "You fool, what's the matter?" His answer from the frightened fellow was. "There's a bloody rat down there."

Yes, and that's the way a lot of us think. We are more concerned with trifles than we are over the things that will blow us into eternity.

A child in a boardinghouse was told that he must eat prunes. But he said he didn't like them and rebelled against them. The harder they tried to force them into his diet, the more opposition there was to them. But they were determined to conquer him, and they resorted to almost everything to accomplish their purpose. In desperation his menu despot told him one night that if he didn't include prunes in his meal the Lord would be very much displeased. He was told in fact that the Lord might get very angry with him. The night he was told this, while he didn't master enough courage to eat the fruit he was so allergic to, he pondered over his displeasing his Creator. After he had gone to bed, it started to thunder. It shook the house and rattled the windows in a terrific way, and the accompanying lightning almost scared the poor kid to death. He couldn't sleep a wink with all those convulsions of the elements and fireworks going on outside. The poor lad finally threw off the bed clothes and peered out into the weather excitement and in desperation exclaimed, "I didn't eat what they asked me to, but I don't know why the Lord makes such a fuss over a *dish of prunes*."

The Lord doesn't make a fuss over a dish of prunes, but we his children do. Sometimes in our intolerance to others we are in no position to criticize.

Sometimes we get so narrow-minded we could hide behind the edge of a knife, and nobody would be able to find us for a month with a microscope. We get out little hatchets, and how we make mountains out of molehills! Do we see the big things in life or do we get so fussy about matters of no width and breadth that we make ourselves appear a tiny pigmy to the fellow who really thinks?

Mr. Jacob Riis who helped clean up the slums of New York was a great friend of Theodore Roosevelt, our great President. If you'll remember, our friend Teddy at the head of his gallant Rough Riders charged the enemy up San Juan Hill. The Spaniards were slaughtering our boys by the hundreds. They were using that famous Mouser rifle with smokeless powder; we were carrying that old-fashioned Springfield

Winchester using black powder, when every time we pulled the trigger it gave the sharpshooter a perfect mark to shoot at. I remind you, the hill became a slaughter-yard. If this program had continued, our brave army would have been annihilated. Something had to be done. The Spaniards had to be charged and pulled from those holes in the rocks, their nests in the trees and ambush in the bushes. Teddy did the job and planted Old Glory on the top of that bloody hill.

Well, let's get back to our story: We were talking about Mr. Riis, life pal of Roosevelt. One day our friend Riis got a letter from a lady friend. The letter ran about as follows:

> "Dear Mr. Riis:
> There is a story about that as Mr. Roosevelt charged up San Juan Hill he said 'Hell." Dear Mr. Riis, could he have used that word? Please look into the matter and correct the rumor immediately."

The good lady who got so excited received a letter back from Riis about as follows:

> "Dear Madam:
> As Colonel Roosevelt charged up San Juan Hill I don't know whether or not he said 'Hell,' but when I received your letter, I did."

The world is crying louder than ever for us to be tolerant towards the other fellow and his viewpoint. The Crusades are the best example in history of what we stoop to in name of religion. In almost every spot in the world you see the land scarred with the result of man's inhumanity to man.

Not understood. Poor souls with stunted vision
Oft measure giants by their narrow gauge;
The poisoned shafts of falsehood and derision
Are oft impelled 'gainst those who mould age,
Not understood.

Not understood. How many breasts are aching

For lack of sympathy? Ah, day by day,
How many cheerless, lonely hearts are breaking,
How many noble spirits pass away,
Not understood.
God, that men would see a little clearer,
Or judge less harshly where they cannot see,
God, that men would draw a little nearer
To one another! They'd be nearer Thee,
And understood.

Thomas Bracken

STORY THREE

THE RIGHT PULL

In which of these buildings are your boys and girls meeting ? Does the building appeal or repel? Does it pull or does it back-peddle against what you fine sisters are doing? Are you working against odds in the building where you are meeting?

If the building breathes dilapidation and uncleanliness, what are you Primary sisters doing about it? The Presiding Bishopric with full authority of the First Presidency have proclaimed "open season" on the unkept places of worship, and we are waging a war against them. Pressure in a wholesome way from you folks will help us make this war successful.

Someone has said, "Let's be brave enough to face the truth even though it kills us." Then let us face the truth. The truth is that some of the buildings in the Church are so shabby, so unkept, so barn-like, if you please, that you and I "color up," to say the least, when we have to admit they belong to us. And many times it is not that the building was not substantially built, but because it has been left to go to rack and ruin. We are sorry to say that some ward leaders in this respect have "eyes and see not and ears and hear not." Some of them can't see broken windows and panels out of the doors that have been patched with rough-hewn boards. They can't hear the cry the building has made for the last forty years for lead and oil. In some places, in all the history of the structure, there has never been a union of paint and lumber, and the chances are that the chapel will die before a marriage with the paint has been realized.

Now you good Primary workers throughout the Church, our little children are coming to you for guidance, and while you pour out your souls to better their lives, in some of the wards much of your tutorage is blown to the far winds by this adverse building environment we are talking about. Won't you help us to create sentiment in localities where these "dark corner" buildings are, that they might be cleaned up and refreshed with soap, water, paint, and a little touch of landscape? If you ladies of the Church will get up in arms, we'll make history in this matter.

Lest we are misunderstood in the erection and care given chapels and other Church buildings, our Church has been going through a renaissance that is next to glorious. As you drive past them from time to time, see if we are not right in that statement. Some Church centers are little "Gardens of Eden." Some of them are away off the main highways where they are not seen by as many as we would like. The culture and breeding of the people of the community have demanded that their buildings represent their better selves, and in so doing they have educated their boys and girls to appreciate the finer things of life. But with all our pounding and pleading, this *Church pride* hasn't manifested itself in all parts of the Church. The dilapidated chapel repels—it doesn't pull.

This article is not written to give the impression that we expect to have palaces as chapels throughout the Church. We honor the humble meetinghouse, but we want it to be kept clean and have an atmosphere that bids you "come in."

You don't have to drag your children to a well-kept, attractive chapel. Ladies of the Primary of this Church, help us to see that our chapels have *The Right Pull.*

STORY FOUR

"LET'S GO BACK AND GET THEM"

Sometimes when a fellow makes a plea for people to be tolerant, he is apt to open himself for criticism. We all want to be called broad-minded. Bernard Shaw says, "Let's be open-minded, but let's not get in a draft." I want to be kind, I want to make allowances, but I don't "want to get in a draft." Someone has wisely observed, "To tolerate doesn't mean to accept."

I repeat, I want to be understood. I want you to take what I say in the spirit that I give it. I hope it is fundamentally sound.

There was a Scotch gentleman who was sick, and his club members decided to call on him. They thought it wouldn't be proper to visit him without leaving with him some little dainty he'd appreciate. Knowing the human side of this man, on the road down to his home they called and purchased (wrapped up in a bonded bottle) some cherries *pickled in brandy*. Before they left, they wanted him to test out the token of their love and esteem. He smacked his lips and said, "I dinna care a muckle for your cherries, but I sure appreciate the *spirit* in which they are sent." Now you may not like what I am going to say—but I do want you to take it in the spirit it is sent.

There are over thirty-five thousand men on our Church rolls who are not active in the Church above the activities of a

JUST AS MUCH SUGAR IN THOSE WHO HAVE SLIPPED OFF...... LET'S GO BACK AND GET THEM!
BISHOP
AARONIC PRIESTHOOD
LEADERSHIP
THOUGHTLESSNESS
UNKINDNESS
INTOLERANCE
MISUNDERSTANDING
OVER 21
BETTER VISION

priest. And let's go a step further:—a big majority of this vast army is doing very little in the Church. What is the matter?

One of the men who had been a very faithful Latter-day Saint stopped at the Presiding Bishopric grounds. He is a rather frank fellow. (And by the way, I wish sometimes that we had more frank people than we have. There are too many who like to polish apples. The boys say the new way of saying this "polishing apples" is "simonizing Jonathans.") He said, "There is a multitude of people who jump about this Church that you don't see, and, furthermore, because of their frailties you consider them lost and gone. You don't understand them, and sometimes we wonder if you want to understand them." Speaking seriously, this is a challenge. Don't you forget that there are thousands who are good people, too. Maybe they aren't walking quite as straight as some of you people think they should. I wonder if we are as broad-minded as we should be. Do we get our little hatchets out and do we unmercifully knock them because they are not adhering to some of our standards? Yes, we would have ourselves think they have junked their lives because of some of these outward weaknesses.

Sometimes you know it is just human nature, if you have someone near and dear to you with weaknesses about which we are speaking, that because of your regard for them, you want to pull out an umbrella of broad-mindedness to shield those that you love dearly from the rains of undue persecution. Lest you think I am playing this role, I want to say I haven't a child who either smokes or drinks. I have six, and they are all old enough to so indulge if so inclined. I'm not bragging about it. But let me say further that if one of them does break over the traces in this regard, though it would break my heart, I hope my arms become that much longer so I can stretch them out and pull my children to me. I hope then that they feel my heart beat in their behalf even stronger than it beats for them now.

Now, just because a man does smoke, do you think you are going to heaven and he is going to the regions below? Maybe you are going to get the surprise of your life when you wake up. Your great slumber may last longer than you expect, and if you don't shape your destiny in the bigger things in life, you'll see him fitted up in apartments in the kingdom to come that will take away your breath.

Do you ever look under a man's coat to find what kind of heart beats there? Or do you just take some of that outside stuff and say "I am all right, and the Lord pity him."

I think the following story comes from one of our good judges of Salt Lake City: A young man came before the judge. He had ruined several girls, and he had stolen right and left. The good mother came to the judge and said, "Notwithstanding what you know, Judge, my boy is a good Latter-day Saint. He doesn't smoke, he doesn't chew, and he doesn't drink tea or coffee.'

I don't know how you size this situation up, but if they would make a vat and fill it with whisky and let that little "stinker" swim in it, it would be a godsend to him, wouldn't it? That is, if it would vaccinate him from his real wickedness, and provided he didn't get out on the highway.

I thought a lot of Henry Taggart, the United States detective. He was always the bodyguard of the President of the United States when he came here. Henry wasn't very particular about his choice of words sometimes, but his heart was such that he was loved by thousands. Yes, he was loved because he was frank. May I pay tribute to that man. I met him at the D. & R. G. Railway station one night as he was about to take the train for Nevada. His going there reminded him of an experience. He told me the story.

A sheriff in the little village had passed away, and Henry had been wired to come down and speak at the funeral. As he stepped to the platform of the little railroad station one of the gentlemen, (you find them throughout the land, who was sure he had a through non-stop ticket to the realms on high) stepped up to him and said, "My, how I pity you to have to talk at this funeral today." May I say here, from what Henry told me this sheriff had some of these weaknesses we are talking about. But Henry knew about the virtues of this fellow that were more than skin-deep, and that's why he had answered the wire and come five hundred miles to say a few words in his behalf. Henry straightened up, and his eyes flashed righteous indignation as he told me of one experience of the gentleman they were about to lay away. On one occasion Taggart had come down to this Nevada county to arrest a "killer." We take his own words, "We HAD to get him. We knew where he was, and the three of us went out to get him, including this man who was being buried. We found the house and were sure he was there. I spoke up and said, 'Now this is my responsibility. You men stay on the outside, and I will go in and get him.' And this sheriff said, 'My dear Henry, you won't go in; I am the fellow who is going in. You have a family, you have a wife and children—I haven't. Here I go.' This man went up to the house, willing to give his life for his fellow man." What did Christ say?—That no man is greater than the man who would give his life for another. Why is your life safe, why can I sleep at night knowing my property is safe from an outlaw? Just what is the price of liberty? How do we get it? Because there are sheriffs who have the stamina and fortitude to lay down their lives for you and me.

Now let me tell you an old story. I am thinking of Civil War times. When the first shot was fired at Fort Sumter, there was a man who was bound to rise, and he was getting seventy-five dollars a month as a clerk. (But I am ahead of my story.) Now, Lincoln was in the depths of the Civil War. He, too, was called the "man of sorrows." He held in his hands your destiny and mine. Another shot was heard around the world; yes, a few million shots were heard around the world in that conflict. "Now we are engaged in a great Civil War, testing whether that nation or any nation so conceived (in liberty) and so dedicated can long endure." Those who did any thinking knew that the war had to be won and won only one way. (I speak respectfully of the South.) This thing had to be fought out. He first had as head of the Union forces this man McClellan. He strutted up and down and paraded but did not "cut the mustard." It was told that Lincoln stood out by his tent one day waiting for an hour to get a word with the general. Lincoln afterward said, when he was criticized for waiting so long at the tent of an inferior, "I would hold his horse if it would just get into battle." But he didn't. Then came Fighting Joe Hooker. He didn't do anything. Then came Burnside. Finally we come to Gettysburg, and if you folks want to see a sight to thrill you to the core, see the battlefield of Gettysburg; see the monument there. But even this man Meade didn't follow through. Even after that battle, the North was worried to death, and this "man of sorrows"—if I may so refer to him—had the worries of a nation on his shoulders and a world's destiny in his hands. But in the meantime this young fellow who was getting seventy-five dollars a month and was a graduate of West Point, gets in the Army. He starts up the Mississippi River. He takes Fort Donelson and Fort Lee, then Vicksburg, and everywhere that fellow moved, his progress was like a ratchet—he held every inch he took. This "man of sorrows" began to breathe more easily. Hope showed up in the battled skies. This man Grant was given command, and Richmond for the first time in three years was in sight. We had to win! But, here come a committee waiting on the President. This man Grant must be removed. Why? Because he was drinking whisky. Lincoln listened to their story and then said, "Gentlemen, if you will please find out what brand he uses, I will send a barrel to each one of the other generals."

We are not through yet. Who was this man Lincoln? He was a man who never touched liquor to his lips. He was the man who got on his knees because there was no other place to go. When you haven't any other place to go, you get on your knees. How did this man Grant lose his life? Every day, almost every minute, he had a cigar in his mouth; as a result he died of cancer of the throat. Did he pay the penalty? Who was this man Grant? One day as a group stood together, one member, anxious to tell an unbecoming story, said, "Are there any ladies present?" Grant spoke up and replied, "There are no ladies present, but there are gentlemen."

Are you big enough, am I big enough, can we be a Lincoln, in a way, to look at a man and, for a minute or two, forget those outward weaknesses; can you see those virtues under his coat? There are men who have weaknesses who will go where you won't go. They fight our battles and make our liberty possible. They have the "intestinal fortitude" to wade in and make our institutions safe.

Did Lincoln mean he would actually send a barrel of that particular "brand" to each of the other generals? He certainly did not! He meant those committee people had lost their sense of values. Lincoln's whole life rebelled against drink. He knew of its evils, but he saw the gold in a man notwithstanding the dross.

I have visited the birthplace of this great man. Just before that angel mother closed her eyes in death she called that raw-boned, nine-year-old lad to her bedside. With her arm around him she kissed a death warning to her boy. "Abe, leave that stuff alone." He did.

On the occasion of his election as president of the United States when men think they have every excuse to relax from the moral rigidity, this big fellow put a pitcher of water on the reception table with an attitude that meant in very deed, "There's Adam's ale. If they don't like it, they can lump it.

There are "Grants" next door to you or in your neighborhood. Do you see the gold or the dross? If we don't see the gold, some day God will.

I would like to make a plea with myself and with you:—Let us be broad-minded. We don't need to get in a draft. Let us have more of the milk of human kindness, Don't let's think that we are saved because we take care of some of those outward things.

"Let's go back and get them."

STORY FIVE

DO YOU DARE TO BE HUMAN?

Lincoln, the great champion of the common people. May what he stood for in emphasizing the virtues of being really human never die.

On one occasion when president, he was found polishing his boots. A stranger seeing this unusual performance by so distinguished an individual exclaimed, "But, Mr. President, do you black your own shoes?" He replied, "Whose shoes do you suppose I'd black?"

How that fellow who stood six feet four inches in his stocking feet loved the following poem by William Knox!

> Oh! why should the spirit of mortal be proud?
> Like a swift-fleeting meteor, a fast-flying cloud,
> A flash of the lightning, a break of the wave,
> Man passeth from the oak and the willow shall fade,
> Be scattered around, and together be laid;
> As the young and the old and the low and the high
> Shall moulder to dust and together shall die.
> 'Tis the wink of an eye; 'tis the draught of a breath,
> From the blossom of health to the paleness of death,
> From the gilded saloon to the bier and the shroud;
> Oh! why should the spirit of mortal be proud?

A short time ago a member of the First Presidency attended a banquet in one of our stakes. Most of the leaders of the stake were there, and with them were their wives or husbands. To use an expression that most of us seem to understand, that authority in mingling with this group let his hair down, and, without losing his dignity, was one with them in their pranks and healthy follies and showed himself to be about as full of human nature as they were. Following that occasion could be heard in this quarter and that quarter, "Wasn't he human?"

Dear officer of this Church, dear magistrate: Church, civic, or what not, your people do everything but pray that you will be human. Many people lose their prestige because they think they've got to be "somebody what they ain't." People will love you for what you are. They want you to be your dear self. Some places where we go, the air is so stuffy with sham that we are all happy to escape to the open breezes of freedom—freedom from pretense. I would think even the kings and queens of the earth are happy when they can take off their long robes and paraphernalia for the occasion, roll up their sleeves, and sit down to the table of anti-tension.

This man Captain Walter T. Stewart of the U. S. Air Forces because of his international recognition for bravery and skill was invited to call upon the queen and her daughters in England. Of course those close to him, realizing what sacred stairs he was going to be treading, had coached him for all he was worth. They didn't want him to break the slightest rule of etiquette. They wanted him to dot every "I" and cross every "T" while he would be standing at attention in the realms of English pomp and aristocracy. He was going to be on the spot, as it were. The whole world would be watching him in every move of his little finger.

Well, the tense moment finally arrived. He was ushered into the presence of the queen and the princesses of Great Britain. I suppose he was getting along okay. He had remembered all his instructions thus far, and he was now confronted with the daughters of the king. Whether he had forgotten the exact hair-breadth salutations or not, I don't know, but on getting the eyes of these lovely young women, he just forgot where he was. The genuine Yankee naturalness overcame him. With real genuine American freedom he walked across the room, smiled at the ladies, and extended his hands to receive an old-fashioned handshake. As he greeted them and shook their hands, as natural as spontaneous combustion, these friendly words burst forth from him: "Girls, how are you? I'm surely glad to meet you."

That day that young officer in the courts of the Great British Empire made a hit. He wanted to be natural—so did they. He was—they were. There is more meaning than one in Patrick Henry's famous words, "Give me liberty or give me death." I suppose there are occasions when we would rather face death than fit into an endless procession of needless red tape.

The funny part of this business is that the bigger the man the easier he is to approach. Very often it is less difficult to get on speaking terms with the king than it is with his servants. As a boy I remember well the observation of a returned missionary from Sweden. He told us that the king was very sociable, but that you couldn't get within ten feet of the king's help.

> Ye see yon birkie ca'd a lord,
> Wha struts, and stares, and a' that,—
> Tho' hundreds worship at his word,
> He's but a coof for a' that;
> For a' that, and a' that,
> His riband, star, and a' that;
> The man of independent mind,
> He looks and laughs at a' that.

Did you ever hear what prompted the poet to write those words? He was called to the Edinburgh Castle as a bard to entertain the nobility of the land. He had waited in an anteroom to be called. As the time rolled on and he waited and waited, his Scotch blood leaped in a' his veins as he listened to their vain carrying on. Through the door he saw their "tinsel show, and a' that." He saw their "riband, star, and a' that."

Poet Bobbie wore "hodden-gray" and "on hamely fare" he dined. In his disgust waiting to be called to entertain the lords of creation, he wrote those words that if he hadn't written anything else in his life would have made him famous.

Those aristocrats today are all forgotten. The lad that followed the plough and was obscure in his toils and a' that today lives in the hearts of millions who call his name blessed because he dared to be human.

"The rank is but the guinea's stamp,—The man's the gowd for a' that." No man who graced the earth knew that better than President Abe Lincoln. One day one of noble birth was ushered in to him. His titles and formal family decorations took a good part of a page when written. As Lincoln grasped the arrogant fellow's hand, he gave him that friendly smile, and with a sly little twist of his democratic mouth he said something like this: "You are welcome, and we'll try to see that your titles will not be held against you."

Few men in American life have emphasized this human side more than beloved Will Rogers. His words, "I never met a man I didn't like" will never die.

We had the pleasure on one occasion to have in our humble home Richard Bonelli, the great American singer. In his presence you feel perfectly at home. He is just one of you. He acted in our home as though he were an old neighbor. I remember the night he was singing for us in the home. He wanted a drink of water. Instead of making his desires known, he walked into the kitchen, took a glass from the cupboard, and helped himself to the city water mains. We like this great artist not only for his wonderful voice but also because he is so human.

No one likes a person who puts on airs. I think my friend Nephi Jensen put it right when he used the words in paying compliment to one he loved: "He's just what he is and no "isser."

When I see someone putting on this air of aristocracy, I think of the negro and his wife eating in a very high class eating house. They were right up in "G", and they wanted those sitting near them to note their culture. They were eating with the tips of their fingers and swallowing each little bite with all the precision of preciseness. They had eaten only a portion of each course. (If they had been home in their own kitchen, they would have had three servings.) When about to the last course the waiter, bowing low, asked her excellency what more could be served. She, with nose extended replied,

"I have had an excellent sufficiency." Then the waiter went to the other party in crime of this little farce. He had not heard distinctly what his good wife had ordered, but he was going to take a chance on more real sophistication. As the waiter bent low in his direction he, with all the dignity in the world, replied, "Please give me the same with a little mustard on."

People who dare not be human will bear watching. The Lord pity them when they are alone.

To thine own self be true; And it must follow, as the night the day, Thou canst not then be false to any man.

Be sure to be yourself. The world will love you if you are human.

STORY SIX

STOP! LOOK! LISTEN!

If you are satisfied with a broken-down building, one that suggests crudeness, that is what you will get. If you demand a properly kept house of worship, one that suggests refinement and an atmosphere that breathes the spirit of worship, you will get it. Demand the best, and the best will come to you. Stand for slipshod janitorial service, and you will sit in dust. "Let's be ourselves, but let's be our better selves."

Sometimes the impression is given that because our pioneers went through untold hardship incidental to frontier life this is the only kind of life they knew. This is just as far from the truth as anything could be. The majority of the pioneers were people of refinement and culture. They appreciated the finer things. To prove this, one has only to go back over the trail and see in the architecture of their homes and church buildings what their character was. Of the Kirtland architecture, Mr. Thomas O'Donnell, A.I.A., assistant professor of architecture at the University of Illinois, says in part:

> Although there are in the world many temples, cathedrals, and churches of architectural and historical interest, yet of all these there is none more unique architecturally or more interesting historically than the "temple" which these Latter-day Saints built in the village of Kirtland.

Mr. A. Leicester Hyde, a district officer in the western states for the Historic American Building survey, made these comments about early Utah architecture after visiting the territory, looking for historic buildings of worth built prior to 1860:

> There are more buildings of historic and architectural merit in Utah than in all the remaining ten western states combined. In New Mexico we have a few mud haciendas; in Wyoming, Fort Bridger, and in California, the Spanish missions.

But in Utah he found a reproduction of New England. He was surprised to find a "Captain's Walk" on the Bee-Hive House, which is a typical New England feature of architecture.

The Authorities of the Church, including the Presiding Bishopric, have been pleading for many years for buildings that really represent us. We are afraid many times that they do not speak of our better selves; and yet, with all this hammering, there are some wards and stakes of the Church that are not responding to our pleading. The two photos opposite are of the same building. One picture represents our better selves, and the other shows how we can get "down at the heels" when we neglect our buildings. A situation of this kind doesn't necessarily reflect the faults of the custodian or even the bishop alone. If the Church members stand for conditions like the first picture, we will have them. If we "spunk up" like the fine people of this ward did, we can change the environment of our boys and girls. One picture suggests dilapidation and the "don't care" attitude, and the other gives the feeling of worship.

Now, here are some of the things you, as a Church member, have a right to demand:

Attitude of the Bishopric. You have a right to expect of your bishop that he sees that the building is carefully inspected from time to time, that all parts of the building are neat and clean and function properly. The bishop should dignify the custodian and see that he receives the cooperation of the ward in helping the custodian keep the building in good condition. A custodian is helpless without proper sentiment.

Attitude of Custodian. You have a right to expect that the custodian be thoroughly clean but also that he be congenial. There is nothing that upsets a ward more than a grouchy custodian.

The Building. You have a right to expect that the building shall be painted inside and out from foundation to roof from time to time. You, as a member of the Church, should know that for several years the Church has offered to pay for the paint if the local people will put it on.

Grounds. There are a few spots in the Church where water for landscaping is not available. Where it is or where the water is accessible with some labor and cost, you have a right to ask that the grounds be properly landscaped, that a few evergreens pierce the sky, and flowers, shrubs and trees adorn the grounds. These help us to worship God as we ought and help us to be reminded of our better selves, culture, and refinement. You have a right to rise in indignation when the grounds show lack of care, and weeds are allowed to grow. You have a right to insist that broken windows be replaced.

Furnishings. You have a right to expect floors to be painted or covered with carpet, linoleum, mastipave, or some covering that eliminates as much noise as possible, so that you will not be disturbed during the time of worship. You have a right to demand that obsolete furniture chiseled with age or jack knives be repaired or thrown out of the chapel. When our pioneers arrived, they immediately had to put up log homes for shelter. They had to make some of their furniture of the crudest type. That day is past. Nothing is more disturbing than to go into some of the Church buildings and see clumsily fashioned furniture for our boys and girls to sit on.

Rest rooms. Nothing is more disgusting than the conditions in some of these rooms in our churches. You have a right to expect the fixtures in these rooms to be constantly in a state of good repair. You have the right to demand that the toilets be properly ventilated, clean, and sanitary. You have a right to expect that there be in these rooms, soap, towels, toilet paper. There should be mirrors. These rooms should be spick and span, and where it is in keeping with the rest of the building, especially in the ladies' rooms, a few touches to the rooms in the way of draperies should be added. These improve the general atmosphere of the building.

Heating and Ventilation. You have the right to expect that the building be properly heated and ventilated, and in some sections it is just as important to have the building cool in the summer as it is to have it warm in the winter.

Fire Hazards. You have the right to expect that the building shall have as low a fire risk as possible. Fire fighting equipment should be placed throughout the building. This should be checked properly from season to season.

In conclusion, it is not intended in this article to intimate that all of our meetinghouses shall be palaces. We are emphasizing order and cleanliness and trying to impress our people that they should and must expect of the authorities of their ward the proper care and furnishing of the places of worship. Never in the history of the Church have we been more mindful or grateful of the sacrifices made by the members of this Church in having proper places for worship, recreation, and education. We don't want to emphasize the negative. We shall be criticized if we do. Where there is a "don't care" attitude, if this article helps to blast it out, it will serve its purpose. The Church will continue to demand better places of worship as represented in the accompanying photographs.

STORY SEVEN

Whenever you think of initiative, grit, pluck, sand, and any of their near relatives, if you have a mental picture of a spider, I suppose the world will forgive you. I cannot think when I first heard of Robert Bruce and the spider. It must have been one of the first stories my mother ever told me. Dear Reader, is that about your experience?

It is just possible that I have been to that very cave where our famous King Robert lay discouraged and got his shot in the arm by the spunk of that spider. I have been in those caves where old Rob Roy, the Robin Hood of Scotland, hid, fighting for the liberty of his people.

Bruce had been kicked badly, and he was all in. They were hunting him with bloodhounds. As he lay there on his back looking up into the ceiling of that rock compartment, his eye caught that spider trying to attach himself to a beam in the cave. He failed twice. The third time he made it. Said Bruce to himself, "If the spider can do it, so can I." He pulled himself together, and with the help of one loyal band after another he gave liberty to Scotland at the Battle of Bannockburn.

Now since that day hundreds of years ago every mother has seen fit to plant "stick-to-it-ism" in her children by reciting that story and telling them of the industry and pluck of this animal that builds his web.

A certain gentleman whose disposition was a mixture of scientist and Doubting Thomas had heard the story of Bruce and the spider and of the unbelievable virtues of the little animal in "get there or die" philosophy. He determined he would find out for himself if the spider really had these things "on the ball" or whether it was all a fairy tale. Yes, he was going to put the famous insect to the test. He did. Whether he performed the experiment on a table in the kitchen or outside in the garden, I don't know. He made a pool of water a foot or less wide, drove a little stake in the middle of the improvised lake, and then, if you please, put our famous little bug on the top of said stick of wood. Mr. Spider was shipwrecked, and on an island, in the same predicament as a Robinson Crusoe. This whole program was worked out to see what that spider would do in an emergency. (What you and I do, Mr. Reader, when we are up against it tells what kind of stuff we are made of.) Now let's see just what the hero of the Bruce story did. He couldn't swim, that's the one thing he couldn't do, but he had to do something or die on that island. He traveled up that pole in the water a time or two. He was apparently getting his bearings and doing some thinking. He came down the mast only to climb up again. He stayed on the top a minute or two. He extended one of his arms and then the other. He might be trying to find in which direction the breeze was going—out to sea or from the sea. That's exactly what he was trying to determine. From his movements he was now satisfied. His observer didn't have to wait long. He pulled himself together for the act You know a spider throws from his body a flood that when it drys is several times stronger than the same amount of steel, yes, including watch springs. He had discovered the movements of the air. With a deadly aim at a little twig or object across the water, in harmony with the breeze, he emitted from his body that substance that would make his suspension bridge to delivery. The gluey thread hit the mark and attached itself to the spot. The tightrope was there Our bridge mechanic put his arms on the wire, flipped it for strength. He found it good—it held his weight. He marched off to safety.

The spider had proved worthy of his reputation. He was weighed in the balance and was not found wanting. The sand and the grit were there, and so was the initiative.

If some people had an idea all of their own, they would call for aspirin for a week. In this day of oceans of books and avalanches of education, if we are not careful, we're going to rely on what somebody else has thought rather than do our own thinking. These days you can do everything but get an idea from a capsule. Undoubtedly, our feats of engineering are greater than at any time in the history of the world, and the inroads we are making on the worlds unknown in science are phenomenal. A person would be rather stupid if he couldn't see it, but I'm still worrying about the initiative of our boys and girls. Elbert Hubbard's essay "Message to Garcia" will live long upon the land. How many of us could land as Rowan did on a dense island, on his own steam, as it were, to deliver the message. As Hubbard puts it, "Are we lost at sea in the ordinary responsibilities of life if we don't have eternally at our elbows a hundred people to answer our questions and direct every move we make?"

When contemplating long hauls in a lumber yard business, especially since the days of the automobile for delivery, one gets a fairly good chance to study men and how they react in an emergency. Some men when the unusual happens get on a telephone and sit and wait for the wrecking crew. Other men, spider fashion, find a way out and deliver the goods.

I shall never forget one day when two men left Salt Lake each with a big load of lumber for a fifty mile delivery through the mountains and over the summit. The reason I remember that day is because both men on the summit ran into about the same kind of grief. You know life sometimes goes in parallels. This day was one of those days. One truck driver slumped—the other rose to the occasion. One driver sent word back to his company by a passer-by and sat the whole day long waiting for help. The other little fellow, bless his soul, (when I think of his pluck my blood pressure of affection rises in his direction) had a terrific load. As he hit the top of the summit, one of the main springs broke, letting the heavy load smash on his axle and crowd the tires. The load had to be lifted. He was equal to the occasion. He too could have sent back for the repair department, but he was determined to deliver the message to Garcia—deliver that load of flooring to the customer who had been promised delivery at a certain time. He knew too that that lumber was sold on a close margin and that every minute of delivery time counted. To shift that load from the tires he had to have a piece of timber. He noted in the distance an abandoned telephone pole with a crosspiece accompanying the same. He climbed to the top of the upright, hammered off the 4 by 6, jacked up his load, placing the timber to take the load. To make the story short, because of his "never die" attitude, three thousand feet of lumber was delivered that day within one hour of schedule. He returned, having delivered his "Message to Garcia."

That little fellow would go through Hades and high water before he'd disappoint his employer. God bless his kind. Having men and women in an organization with loyalty and spunk makes business a pleasure.

I went to a Scottish reunion recently. Some fellow just newly across from his native land told a story that has stuck to me like glue. Here it is as nearly as I can remember it.

After Lord Nelson had "steamed" into the Mediterranean and arranged his fleet to meet the combined Spanish and French fleets at Trafalgar the next morning, he called on board of his flagship all the captains of his numerous boats. They were all arranged on the deck of that ship waiting for inspiration from that great English admiral. He looked into the whites of their eyes and gave forth those famous words that decorate the best pages of the most sacred literature, "England expects this day that every Englishman shall do his duty."

There were on board Nelson's ship two Scotchmen, each a commander of a boat that was to play its part in making history the next day. The Scotch always get together, so naturally these two fellows of the land of the heather were standing side by side. When Nelson gave forth those words, one of the Scots about whom we are speaking nudged the other with this observation, "Ye ken he didna mention the Scotch." His companion was ready for him. He poked him back in the ribs. "*The Scotch dinna need to be telt.*"

They had a clear understanding that day between them that the Scotch don't need to be told. Young man, young woman, one of the finest things that can be said of you is that you do your own thinking and don't have to be told. Parents, I repeat, the greatest birthright you can hand down to your children is self-reliance. This self-reliance is something in the way of inspiration which you have instilled into their bones that leads them through life with this war cry, "Sink or swim, survive or perish, I'll take my responsibility." Yes, I like this one, "They depend upon me—I'll be there."

Parents, don't do the thinking for your children. Let them stand on their own feet.

Almost everyone has read the story *Ivanhoe*. Do you remember the story of the tournament and how the Black Knight saved Ivanhoe? King Edward the Third was his father. May his name go down in history as a game father. He believed that the only way you can put steel up a boy's back is by throwing responsibility on him and letting him do his own maneuvering. Let me hit the highspots of that story.

King Edward determined upon an invasion of France. He took over with him nearly one thousand ships and thirty thousand men. Among these warriors was the king's son who was just over fifteen years of age. This lad knelt on the sands of France, his father touched his shoulder with the sword, and this young fellow arose to his feet a knight. He must now win his spurs. His game father had chosen this fight with one hundred and twenty thousand French, four to one odds, for the occasion when his son was to win his spurs.

We shan't go into too much detail. Edward picked the battleground. The followers of France were eager to meet him and were happy to make the charge headed by the king of France himself. I said the king of England that day was a gamester. Let's see if he was. He put his son, the Prince of Wales, surrounded by his generals, in the front ranks to take the brunt of the battle. He as much as said to his son, "Now the battle is yours. I am out of it. You're a knight—let England see this day what kind of stuff you are made of."

And that isn't all. King Edward withdrew himself from the fight and left it to his son. He climbed to the top of a windmill to observe the battle.

The French with all their fury, four to one, mind you, made the attack. For the moment it looked as if it wasn't going too well with the British and their fifteen year old commander-in-chief. Couriers were sent to the king in the windmill, telling him he had better come and save the day and the life of his son. Please note the comeback of England's chief: "Is my son alive?" "Yes." "Has he been dehorsed?" "No." "Then go on with the battle. Let him win his spurs, for I wish if God so desires that the day should be his and the honor thereof remain to him and to those to whom I have given him in charge."

And the king remained in the windmill. With the help of those terrible English bowmen and the self-reliance put into twenty thousand more, they drove the French from the field and won one of the greatest victories in English history.

That lad left on his own became the famous Black Knight,

and because his father put responsibility on him and left him to work things out for himself he made one of the greatest kings of the greatest Empire in the world.

STORY EIGHT

THE HARD WAY OR THE RIGHT WAY

The **RIGHT** *Way*

Bishop: Are you doing it the Hard Way or the Right Way? Bishop, do you occasionally step aside and watch yourself go by? Will these two sketches help you get away from yourself to really see yourself? If you are doing it the hard way, in the first place, it will kill you off quickly; and in the second place, you are depriving your people of the blessing of team work. "Work for everybody and everybody working" is one of the very best slogans adopted by a ward or stake. There will be occasions when you feel that a certain responsibility, because of your position and because of your experience, had better be done yourself. That is as it should be; that's why you were chosen bishop; but don't forget you are made bigger and more valuable as you delegate authority. Men and women grow by making mistakes. Get the key people of your ward accustomed to making decisions—that's what makes them valuable. Let them know you depend upon them—they'll be there with the goods. It's the same with a ward as it is with a family—a wise father and mother have their children make their own decisions. They stand on their own feet; they "paddle their own canoe." In such an attitude the parents are developing real men and women.

Sometime ago a road builder took a contract to build a road somewhere in Idaho. This contractor had working with him a young nephew—the latter was aggressive, dependable, and full of spunk and, thought his uncle, "I'm going to try him out. I'll see what's really in him. I'm going to put him on his own." The next day the following conversation took place: The uncle said, "Bill, I've just taken a contract to build that twenty-mile road." The boy said, "Unc, that's swell. We'll give her fits, won't we?" The contractor, "Bill, I've been thinking, how would you like me to give you the equipment and men, and you build that five-mile stretch in the valley?" Bill, "Unc, do you think I can?" Uncle, "Bill, I think you can." Bill, "We're on. I'll give her all I've got."

The twenty-mile road was started, and Bill with his men, caterpillars, drags, bull-dozers, was making the rocks fly on the five-mile road. All the ambition and initiative of youth was in high gear. Things were going great; the contractor was happy; so was Bill. Yes, and Bill's men were happy, too. They liked the kid. But life doesn't always run smoothly, neither does road building. It started to rain—all one day—then the next—yes, and the third and fourth days. Everything now was mud and more mud. It was a time contract, and the road must go through. But the more youth and energy displayed itself to get out of the hole, the deeper everything mired. Bill became serious. One caterpillar (let's call it a cat) found itself up to its belly in mud. Bill sent the second cat in to rescue it. The latter found itself up to its hips and helpless. Bill had one cat left, and, lo and behold, in its effort to help out its campanion cats, it too floundered and half tipped over. Now Bill was in real trouble. He knew it, and so did his men. But what made matters worse than ever, at this particular moment, along came the big boss—the contractor of the twenty-mile road. What would he think? What would he say? What would he do? But the boss was a general. The boss was using his head. Just what did he do? With his hands in his pockets, whistling, under full control, he sized up the situation in a jiffy. "Well, boys, you're in a little trouble. I've some myself. Well, good luck." He walked away leaving that fine Bill with his men to get out of the mud *themselves*. They did. It was their responsibility. They got into a huddle, upheld the hands of their kid boss, and went to work. With mud up to their hips, they got busy. The first cat was uprighted, and it started purring; and then the second. The third cat scratched itself out, and the five-mile road was on its way to completion. The boss had said he'd put the boy on his own. He did. He didn't weaken him by helping him get out when he needed to bring into play all his capabilities. Bill now had more confidence than ever in himself. Now Bill could build a twenty-mile road—now his boss could take bigger contracts. Bill could take it.

Help a moth out of his cocoon, and he soon dies. Let him get out himself, and he breaks forth a vigorous, healthy moth. Help weakens.

Next time the family hen sits on a bunch of eggs, the day

they are about ready to break forth into the big old world of ours you just help them come into the world by breaking the shells and see what happens. You will weaken them, maybe kill them.

Bishop, the same philosophy holds good in your ward. Let your members always feel free to come to you for advice, but remember emphatically that while those working with you with prayer in their heart are making decisions, your time may be given to something else. As the old saying goes," It is better to keep ten men working than to be doing ten men's work.

Bishop, lean on the officers and members of the ward, and don't let them lean too heavily on you. It is always better to wear out than rust out, but don't do it the hard way—do it the right way.

Mr. Church leader, whoever you are, are you recognizing with dignity and appreciation the men and women or the boys and girls at your elbow? Are you trying to do the whole job or are you delegating authority to others? Nothing will make your work better and you feel happier than if you will throw responsibility on others. If they make a few mistakes, let's not be too concerned over it. We grow by correcting our errors. That is the way we reach perfection.

STORY NINE

Don't Dam Your Spiritual Garden

The man or woman doesn't live who at least in moments of his life doesn't feel a connection with a Creator of all we are and all we contact in the universe. Yes, I am speaking of Robert G. Ingersoll and Darwin. It has always been the case and probably will be for another hundred thousand years that a fool can ask more questions in a minute than the wisest man in the world can answer in a lifetime. You can't look into a flower; you can't observe an ant doing his regimental duties in connection with his marvelous organization but what you see the hand of the great Architect. Some faithful fellow with a scientific makeup and tremendous ability to work tells us there is in the human body twenty-six billion cells. (Now had he said only twenty billion most of us couldn't very well, with any foundation at all, afford to contradict him.) I repeat, twenty-six billion cells all working in harmony and in a sense in unison to make a man and his functions.

Some great thinker has spoken of the Ruler of the heavens as the Absentee Creator, but that fellow knows in his bones, whether he will own up to it or not, that every fiber of his being prays for a hereafter and a chance over the horizon to live again and enjoy the association of those he loves.

Here is a little humor, but decidedly this little literary snack carries a "wallop" of philosophy: A certain gentlemen with pride in his heart that he was a free thinker and had a mind that did its own deducting, remarked triumphantly to a group of his friends, "My father was an atheist; my grandfather was an atheist; and, thank God I'm an atheist." It sounds something like someone else said recently when he served, "Would to God we could all be atheists, so we could live like Christians together."

Let me go a little further along this line regarding people saying what they do not mean which causes spontaneous combustion in expressions of our inner selves. I heard President David O. McKay tell this experience. I'll try to tell it the way I heard it: President McKay had a dear friend who pretended to be an agnostic. The daughter of the latter had lived with her father so long that she had become saturated with his thinking. Well, this good man died, and he was a good man notwithstanding his mental manipulations had become slightly out of gear. I remind you that the father had been dead when our Church Authority called on the daughter. "Mary," said he, "I would like to do the temple work for your father. Mary, I want your permission, of course, before I do this." Now please note the deep down conviction in the soul of this good woman, convictions she thought she was hiding from the world: "David, that's all right, but don't you do one single thing that in any way will keep me from my father."

Many people with deep hopes and spontaneous beliefs would have others think they had little religion. I had the pleasure a couple of years ago of dining with this man James C. Whittaker, one of those fellows with Eddy Rickenbacker who was stranded in the middle of the Pacific for three weeks. You all know of the hawk story—you know of their first real meal after that ordeal. I am talking about that diet of rats and coconuts. I will not go into details.

After our meal together where they recited many details of their trials and final rescue, I had the pleasure of walking out to the hall from the dining room of the hotel with Mr. Whittaker. In conversing with him I thundered this question at our guest: "Mr. Whittaker, if you don't mind, I'd like to ask you a very pertinent question—pardon me, if it appears impertinent." His reply was, "Shoot." "Mr. Whitaker, was there anything supernatural that came to you gentlemen in your three weeks out in those rubber boats?" He looked me in the face and replied, "I never went to church in my life, but I want to tell you I have two new words in my vocabulary, 'I believe.' We didn't pray to God—we talked to Him. Mr. Ashton, tell me if you can, where the strength came from, after three weeks of starvation, before those wonderful brown men rescued us, to paddle that twelve miles to that island."

That soul Whittaker is like millions in the world—chuck full of religion, but he didn't know it.

If I am taking considerable time here in emphasizing this theory all men have religion, forgive me. The greatest thing in the lives of all of us is our religion. We may disagree on some details of doctrine and the geography over the horizon, but we all want to pray and keep to the best of our ability in tune with what our convictions are. In other words, we all have a spiritual garden.

Now do you, dear reader, keep this garden cultivated? Do you let anyone stand to obstruct you in the fruits of what that garden will yield? So often one sees a person who pretends to be religious do something off-color, and then that person looking on lets that fellow's actions deter him from doing his duty as a man ought to do to cultivate himself spiritually. So often you hear something like this: "If that's what you call religion, I'm through." If a man's a hypocrite, that's nothing to do with religion. Do you, do I, in seeing the faults of others let that hinder you and me from doing our duty? If a fellow pretends to be pious and then pulls a dishonest stunt, he just makes a monkey of himself. If you and I do some real thinking, we just look on and laugh at his shallowness. The roots of that fellow don't go into the ground four inches. Anybody who is just half awake "looks and laughs at a' that." But don't let that fellow "dam your spiritual garden."

Now let's get back to our cartoon. Let me tell you a story I heard at a conference the other day from the lips of Ralph B. Keeler of the Sunday School General Board. That story prompted the artist's drawing in this article.

Brother Keeler said there was a certain bishop, and he was a right good bishop, too, who had some misunderstanding with a certain head of a family in his ward. The bishop had done about everything he possibly could to bring about a better feeling towards himself as the bishop from this particular man. According to the story he said to our friend, "Brother Smith, if there is anything you can suggest that I can do to show you how badly I feel about the situation and that will make you feel better, please let me do it." According to Brother Keeler the bishop had done everything but ask forgiveness from a ward member. In other words, the bishop left no stone unturned in trying to make things right. As it were, he scraped the bottom of the humility and courtesy barrel to show his brother how anxious he was that there be a better feeling between them. In the face of all the bishop could do, the brother out of harmony with his bishop stood out defiantly and resisted any overtures of the bishop. Of course, when the head of a family is out of harmony with his leader that cancer distributes itself all through the family. The wife wouldn't come out to Church, and even the children stopped coming to Sunday School. The whole atmosphere was filled with bile because of this situation between the father of the ward and the father of those children. The bishop went to the 'phone one day and called our rather obstinate brother and asked as a special favor that the gentleman come to his office. Our friend responded, and he and the bishop met. Then our good bishop made this observation:

"Brother Smith, last night I had a dream. I want to relate it to you. I dreamed I saw a beautiful valley. In that valley were the most beautiful farms in the world, all irrigated and kept irrigated by a beautiful mountain stream. I saw the owner of these beautiful farms in controversy with the watermaster. The harder the watermaster tried to administer the water equitably and fair the more stubborn was the owner of this particular farm.

"Brother Smith," continued the bishop, "I saw the men

all but get into a battle royal. In the face of all the watermaster could do the owner of this particular farm in question tightened his fists and said, 'As long as you are watermaster, I won't use a drop of your water.' Brother Smith, I saw his beautiful farm start to wilt. It first got the small stuff, then the bushes, and yet in spite of all of this our vehement friend still shook his fists and refused to take the water. In the dream I saw the trees finally fold up, and in a couple of years time I saw what was formerly a little Garden of Eden spot turned into a piece of scorched desert. The water was still there; the distribution was there to give to this man his portion, but because of enmity between him and the watermaster his farm went back to a barren waste."

If I remember the story correctly, the good member of the ward having this trouble with the bishop dropped his head and said, "Bishop, I believe it is our move. We will be to Church next Sunday."

Now I think that story has an application in what we are talking about. I say, "Is there someone standing between you and your spiritual growth?" That man's whole family was suffering spiritual drought because the father was out of tune with the bishop of his ward. Are you, dear reader, because of some personality difference between you and those over you or those working with you, going to let your spirituality dry up?

If we expect the blessings of heaven, we must anticipate a program of a continual flow of spiritual water, as it were, the same as we expect our gardens to be kept green by the contact they have with the irrigation system. Some of us get it in for John Jones because he has some weaknesses, and then because of these weaknesses we get stubborn, set our teeth, and let our souls dry up. If a man in a position is living anything but a consistent life, just wait long enough and someone will catch up with him, and the Lord surely will.

May I use a little rough expression here used by Lorimer who wrote *Letters of a Self-made Merchant to His Son?* "Hot air can take a balloon a long way, but it can't keep it there. In the end there always comes a time when the parachute doesn't work."

Sometimes we find the healthiest family in the world spiritually, and something comes along in the way of personalities, and the first thing you know a weed gets hold of them, and they feed on it until their lives are ruined.

While in Scotland I met a dear gentleman whose blood was saturated with the corpuscles from Ireland. He had a sense of humor and a pack of good stories that he often threw out at the right time. I will never forget this story:—

He said a farmer had a beautiful heifer. She was a blue-ribbon animal. He made up his mind when that calf grew up it would be the prize winner of the country. He did everything humanly possible for that animal in safeguards, proper food, so that she would develop into the animal he wanted her to be. He put her in a pasture all by herself with the sweetest of grass up to her knees. He wanted the atmosphere and everything, combined with a right diet, to put into that calf the virtues of a real animal. When he put her in the field, she was slick and fat, but he noticed a week later in visiting the field where the animal was that she was hardly in as good trim as the day she entered the pasture. He kept observing her, and in spite of the wonderful grass and environment he noticed that she was failing in her weight. The light in her eyes started to fade. After three or four weeks he was so alarmed that he made up his mind to make an investigation. He proceeded accordingly. He examined every foot of this new acreage in which he placed her. He was almost beside himself when he found the trouble in the corner of the pasture. He watched her proceedings, and the next day he found she would fill up with the nutritious grass in the morning, and in the afternoon after her noon drink she would go up to the corner of the pasture and start licking at a terrible weed located there. This weed was destroying all the vitamins she was getting from good food that he had been so careful to arrange.

Yes, many of us children stand knee high in God's blessings, and instead of waxing strong and realizing our full stature we dwindle to pigmies because we feed on a noxious weed in the corner of our pasture. When I use the word "weed," I mean that silly something in us that lets some individual stand in the way of our spiritual growth. Meet him face to face, banish to the far winds your differences, or plough around him and keep in tune with the infinite.

Don't dam your spiritual garden.

STORY TEN

BISHOP: WHAT IS YOUR SENSE OF VALUES?

In other words, Bishop, "do you see gold in them thar hills?" When Colonel Jackling surveyed the sandy hills to the west of Salt Lake City, his sense of values told him that hidden therein were millions in copper. It doesn't take much intelligence, when gold is flashed in your face, to realize that you are beholding a precious metal, but what is important is to discern value when it is obscured or hidden. The virtues of grace and beauty were hidden in the awkward clumsy personality, if you please, of the Ugly Duckling. Jumbo, the elephant, was loved by the millions of children of Great Britain for a generation or two. He was world renowned for his almost unbelievable dimensions, but he was once the scrub of the herd. It took a P. T. Barnum to see this hidden value. Now look at the awkward unsymmetrical, unpromising colt in this picture. Bishop, have you noticed a young thoroughbred—how all out of proportion he appears—long, awkward-looking legs and over-sized knee joints? When you looked him over, were you impressed that in a couple of years such a specimen would make a Man of War, slipping off a mile in one minute and thirty-seven seconds?

We are still talking about hidden values, but what we want to emphasize here are not horses, swans, and elephants, but things decidedly more precious, *boys and men*. Yet, the above comparisons may help us to keep in mind eternally that sometimes a boy's outward appearance may throw us off the track in appreciating those hidden values that perform such miracles. This unkempt, awkward product of the frontier, (in accompanying illustration) sprawled on the floor putting into his head every piece of knowledge and inspiration from the pages of a book read by the flickering light from the open fireplace—who would have had the audacity to prophesy that that same piece of humanity in that log cabin would forty years later sign a document that would break the chains of bondage of three million of his fellows? Who would have dreamed that that same fellow would some day give a three-minute talk that would be heard around the world, and every letter of it be cut in stone and cast in bronze, throughout the civilized world?

Bishop, do you see those values under that mat of unkempt hair sticking through the straw hat of an American boy? Bishop, do you have the discernment to see behind the inquisitive mischievousness of an Edison the world light-flooded with an incandescent lamp? Bishop, it was that kind of stuff that gave you James Watts, the Ben Franklins, your Lindberghs, and MacArthurs. If you see the possibilities of that lad over whom you preside, you'll love him that much more—and if you love him, we don't worry about the rest of it.

The following poem has been quoted, but it probably has not appeared before in print. At one of our general conferences, one of the Authorities referred to a boy as being like a zipper. David H. Elton, a prominent member of the Church and at the time mayor of Lethbridge, Canada, caught the zipper idea and wrote this poem. It hits the nail on the head in this philosophy we are stressing. We compliment him for the genius of the piece of its soundness.

ZIPPERS AND BOYS

The zipper's a modern contraption,
Supplanting the "button" and "lace,"
We now bid "good-bye" to the "hook" and the "eye;"
The zipper has taken their place.
It travels on delicate meshes,
And fastens quite snugly and tight,
If you wish it to work, don't give it a jerk,
But pull it through—smoothly and light.
Now, boys are just somewhat like zippers—
If you jerk them, they get off the track,
And you're likely to find you're left 'way behind,
And cannot move forward or back.
You're balked and stranded, I fear,
For it's a dead cinch you can't move an inch
When your meshes are all out of gear.
If you'll just treat the boys like a zipper
And start them out right—they'll come through,
And nine times out of ten will make splendid men—
Energetic, efficient, and true.
But thrust them, and twist them, and jerk them—
Like the zipper, they'll slip out of clutch,
And you've stalled that dear boy—your hope and your joy—
The lad that you valued so much!

—D. H. Elton

STORY ELEVEN

THE PLOUGHBOY

"Yesterday I rode horseback past a field where a boy was plowing. The lad's hair stuck out through the top of his hat; his form was bony and awkward; one suspender held his trousers in place; his bare legs and arms were brown and sunburned and briar-scarred. He swung his horses around just as I passed by, and from under the flapping hat-brim he cast a quick glance out of dark, half-bashful eyes, and modestly returned my salute. His back turned, I took off my hat and sent a 'God bless you' down the furrow after him. Who knows? I may go to that boy to borrow money yet or to hear him preach or to beg him to defend me in a lawsuit; or, he may stand with pulse unhastened, bare of arm, in a white apron, ready to do his duty while the cone is placed over my face and life or death comes creeping into my veins. Destiny awaits just around the corner. Be patient with the boys."

Boys and men are just the same. Do you see greatness behind that red hair sticking through that straw hat that even the Deseret Industries would put into the bonfire? Do you see that thoroughbred underneath all that unkempt nature-in the-rough? Do you see anything great held together with one suspender and an eight-penny nail instead of a button? Do you see the pumping of that loyal heart underneath the battered sweater and threadbare coat? Bobbie Burns put it better than I can:

> What tho' on hamely fare we dine,
> Wear hoddin gray, and a' that?
> Gie fools their silks, and knaves their wine,—
> (Now change it just a trifle)
> That boy's the man, for a' that!

To put it concretely: If you had stood on the same street in Philadelphia that day, down which marched a lad of twelve or fourteen arriving from Boston "on his own"—with part of a loaf of bread sticking out of one pocket and his socks and shirt dangling from the other—would you have had the sense of values to announce to the world, "There goes the unpresentable kid that will be one of the greatest statesman and geniuses of his time and one of the real founders of this great republic?" The world loved Ben Franklin.

Suppose you were riding on that train in the express car of which a lad was getting his ears boxed for spilling phosphorus on the car floor in his youthful experiments in chemistry. Would you have had the sense of values to surmise that those ears so boxed by the brakeman were the cause of deafness in later life to the greatest electrical wizard of all time—Thomas Edison? Would you have had the sense of values to discern that that fellow caught in the middle of the night would some day give to the world over a hundred major inventions fiddling with electric wires?

I ask you, folks, could you see in a humbly clad sheepherder on the desert plains of Palestine the faith to plug with a stone from a sling the forehead of a giant, and afterwards become one of the greatest kings of all time?

To repeat again, the trouble with us parents and we who have to do with young boys is that we don't look at the boy and see values ahead. We think more of our business interests than we think of him. We think more of our herds than we think of him.

A boy came to his mother sometime ago and said as follows: "Ma, why is it that when dad's pup gets sick he races up to the drugstore and stays up all night nursing that pup with poultices and medicine? Pa really worries over that pup when he gets sick. Ma, when I get sick, all dad does is roll over and groan." Now the mother had been asked a question by her offspring. She was put right on the spot. She must answer the question. Well, this good mother had a splendid sense of humor. When the question was put to her, with a twinkle in her eye she looked her boy in the face and said, "Bill, the only answer I can give you is that undoubtedly the father of the *pup* is a thoroughbred."

We have a fellow down our way and while he has a big family all he cares about is business. He is in the merchantile business and the things that interest him most are sales, costs, profits. In fact, he gets himself so wrapped up in business all the time that it would seem that the world would come to an end if he gave any time to his children. Of course he is a good provider and he takes care of their clothes and the necessities of life. Well, one day his wife came home about noon and to her surprise she found him at home, but what really astonished her was that there he stood looking steadfastly, intently on the bouncing child in its crib. Never did she remember his giving so much time in gazing so steadfastly into that crib as he was that day. She was overwhelmed with joy. She thought, "Well, John has had a turn for the better. He is really going to be interested in the children." In delight she threw her hands up into the air as he still stood gazing into the cradle. She exclaimed, "Oh, John, a penny for your thoughts!" Notice the answer he gave— "Mary, what gets me is how the devil they can make that cradle for ninety-eight cents."

I would like to tell you a story about a stranger down south who called in to see a farmer who was largely engaged in the raising of pigs. The stranger noticed hogs dodging under every bush. It really looked as if he had a big inventory of pigs around the ranch. The stranger asked, "How many pigs have you here?" Promptly came the reply, "Three hundred sixty-two." Then the stranger asked him how many children he had. He yelled back to the house, "Ma, how many children have we now, nine or ten?" Of course, the wife came back with the right answer. Then said the stranger, "My dear man, what gets me is that you can tell me exactly the number of pigs you have, but you are uncertain as to the number of children you have." Please note the answer—"Mr. Stranger, I want you to understand that every one of those pigs is a thoroughbred."

You can never tell what kind of heart beats in a boy's bosom. Deep down in that boy's anatomy there are heroism and greatness if we could only see them. Shabby clothes and even dirt often hide greatness.

They tell a story of a little victim of the slums, an unkempt lad of about ten. His younger sister was found desperately sick. By some kind hands she was rushed to the hospital and a transfusion was immediately necessary. The next thing, of course, was to find blood that clicked with her blood. They thought the blood of her brother mentioned would likely match. It did. They asked him if he would give his blood for his sister. An hour after this operation he asked the doctor how his sister was doing. The answer came that she was doing well. Now note his answer back:— "But, Doc," says he, "when do I croak?" In other words, when he was asked the question, "Will you give your blood to your sister?" he thought it meant would he would give his life for his sister. Notice how quickly the answer came, "Sure." With all his dirt and rags there burned in his bosom a love that could not be surpassed. Christ said, "Greater love hath no man than this, that a man lay down his life for his friends."

Down the glacier's track from your mountainous home
Rushing madly o'er boulder-strewed bed, head covered with foam,
Now racing and frothing through tree-bedecked glade,
You come gently to rest in a shadowy pool so placid and staid
As the riotous life of tempestuous youth
A mad dash, achieving a dare
Which later may be seen as a delusion and snare;
Oh, would that the sobering wisdom of age
Could guide us in life, through this primitive stage,
To temper our actions and teach us to know
That life at its best is but a mad race,
For true happiness drives at a more moderate pace,
As wisdom will show.

STORY TWELVE

IT GOT A BAD START

Let me tell you a story of this coconut tree. Instead of standing erect, proud of its foliage and fruit, it crawls on the ground, fruitless, like a python snake. What's the trouble? Simple enough—it just got a bad start.

A few years ago it was my pleasure to visit the beautiful land of Hawaii. It's a great land of sights and inspirations. In every nook and corner you find something of unusual interest. Bishop Woolley was ushering me about one day. It was in that territory immediately surrounding the Hawaiian Temple. As we went about inspecting Church property and having new experiences, he remarked to me, "Bishop, there is something over in this estate that will be interesting to you. You won't see such a sight very often. Indeed," continued he, "it's a real freak." I soon saw that he had not exaggerated. There in a beautiful grove of coconut trees sprawled on the ground, as I said, like a reptile, was this brother palm tree. Without free contact with the healthy sea breeze and the sunshine was this creeping thing.

Then came the observation of our bishop guide— "The only trouble with this tree that makes it unlike the rest of his fellows is that when it was taking root, getting ready to lift its head to the sun, somebody gave it a kick. It started like the rest from the coconut itself, but its start was disturbed by a shove from some thoughtless fellow's shoe."

Yes, and what is true of coconut trees is true of human beings, and especially true of boys and men. As you walk through the forests of men, you occasionally see a fellow, instead of his shoulders square and head to the sun, you see an unfortunate specimen crawling on the ground like a snake. What has been wrong? I repeat, it is the result of the movement of some thoughtless shoe leather. Yes, and may I say very emphatically, trying to play on words, (and we all like to so indulge) a result of more leather than brains—a result of more knee action than head.

Go with me on a short mental jaunt. Let's go to one of the prisons. Yes, here you'll see a whole forest of these human crawling coconut trees. That youth in that bastille in the San

Francisco harbor Alcatraz costs you and me seven silver dollars a day, or if his average stay in this institution is thirty years, it just costs the simple sum of seventy-six thousand dollars per boy.

Mr. Dad or Mr. Citizen you who may have some responsibility with that fellow, with the twist of your wrist you shape the destiny of your brother. We recently had a few cars in Salt Lake City running on steel rails. As the car pulled up to the corner of Second South and Main the motorman in charge of this particular vehicle lifted a six foot rod hanging in the front of his car, put the chisel-shaped end in the switch, and with the twist of his wrist he determined the destiny of that streetcar. I repeat, with the twist of his wrist he shaped its destiny--whether it is to go east or west or continue going south.

And with the twist of your wrist, Mr. Dad, you determine to a great extent the course of your boy's life—whether its course shall be into the swamp of degradation or to the heights that a normal boy or man wants to attain. Mr. Dad, in your attitude, if you please, you say whether the human coconut shall loop-the-loop on the ground with no fruits of its existence or stand erect with his fellows, proud of his life.

They tell me there's a little lake in the Yellowstone country that sits right on the great divide—at that point within a stone's throw which determines whether the rainfall shall drain into the Pacific or ultimately plunge two thousand miles away into the Atlantic. A gentle breeze over that lake, which we are talking about, determines whether the water of the lake that day makes its debut into the ocean to the west or the longer journey into the Atlantic.

We are not talking fairy tales—we are talking about real life, and how we see the tragedies as a result of poor manipulation of the *wrist*.

When you want to read a story of an unfortunate lad who became, because of a twist of a wrist, a fortunate fellow, get the book *David Harum*. Find the story of widow Mrs. Cullom. Let me hit the high spots of the story:—

I saw the play on the stage. The curtain goes up. It is a dining room scene on Christmas Eve. The table is set, and you can tell they are expecting company. The front door opens—an old lady trembling from head to foot is ushered in and is seated by the fireplace. She is shaking all over because the big fellow, the horse trader, (the banker of the town), who has invited her to his home tonight holds the mortgage over her head. She thinks he is going to put her out in the cold. A side door opens, and in walks this fellow who holds her destiny in his hands. He greets her with an affection that pretty nearly takes her off her feet. When he has smoothed down her anxiety, he stands before her with a little yellow handkerchief in his hands. As he untwists a corner of same a little silver dime falls to the floor. (Will you let me, dear reader, say in my own words the speech as I remember his giving it to the old lady as he brought her to her feet that night?) "Mrs. Cullom, I called you over tonight to pay to you the dividends of the investment of that ten-cent piece put into my hands years ago. I was a lad of about ten years of age. I had a good father, but all he thought a kid was for was to work. I suppose he hadn't had much pleasure as a boy, and I suppose he didn't think that his boy was entitled to any. Mrs. Cullom, the circus was coming to town the next morning. I got all ready for it, and so did Dad. I got up at 4:00 a.m. to be on the ground when they put up the tent. But Dad beat me to it. That morning he put that hoe in my hands with this threat—'Dave, if I've ever given ya a lickin in your life, that was a pigmy to what you'll get today if you leave those potatoes.' Mrs. Cullom, if ever the tops got chopped off spuds it was that morning. My eyes were going in one direction and the hoe in another. I stood it until the parade passed the farm. When I saw the elephants and the camels and the Arabian horses, the hoe stayed in the field, but I went through the fence. I followed the parade to the circus grounds. I was standing in front of the fellow selling tickets to the side show—my mouth wide open showing a row of butter teeth, my red hair poking through a dilapidated straw hat. I was dead to the world, drinking in the picture of the fat lady and the woman with snakes when a great big hand came down on my head. I thought I was paralyzed. When I came to with enough courage to look up, a great big smiling face opened up on me, and I heard a voice say, 'Honey, would you like to go to the show?' He put my little dirty mit into his big paw, and we went in. We saw all the animals and then went into the big show. He bought me popcorn, circus lemonade, and all the trimmings. And when the show was over, he patted me on the back and bade me good-bye. As I left him, he put a dime into my hand.

"Mrs. Cullom, that was the dime you saw drop to the floor. The owner of that big hand on my head that day, the owner of that big smiling face that opened up on me that day was your husband, Bill Cullom.

"Up to that moment in my life I had an inferiority complex and all the trimmings. That big hand on my head and a voice that burst forth with 'Honey, would you like to go to the show' changed my whole life. All I am I owe to that day when that big hand came down on my head. Mrs. Cullom, Dad made good his promise—I got a lickin', but it was worth it.

"I told God with his help that someday I'd pay the interest on that ten-cent investment. Tonight that is why you're here. Here's the thousand dollar mortgage paid in full with my compliments."

Don't encourage wrongdoing in the youth, but when they

make mistakes let's not magnify them. Let's make some allowances. I know of a town not too far from Salt Lake City where you have a score or more families out of the Church because those boys in an unguarded moment cut up capers on Halloween. They were too rigidly dealt with. The adults responsible for this harshness were swimming that week in an unguarded sea. Those fellows, I understand, were told to ask forgiveness before the body of the Church or be excommunicated. Yes, they are out there in no-man's land because they wouldn't ask for forgiveness—and their posterity is out in that land, too. Sometime somebody will have something to answer for. Somebody blundered. It should have been otherwise.

At a conference some time ago I told the people there this sad Halloween experience. After the meeting a good brother about fifty-five told me this story. He said he couldn't tell his town's people, but he wanted to tell me. Here is the story:—

"About twenty-five years ago my wife and I gave a party. At 11:00 p.m. we went out on the back porch to get the freezer of ice cream we had frozen a couple of hours before. But, when we got there 'the cupboard was bare and the poor little doggie had none.' In other words, the ice cream had taken wings. Bishop, if I'd had those fellows in my hands at the moment of my embarrassment I could have smashed their heads together. But, Bishop, I got hold of myself—I stepped back and counted to ten. Do you know what I did? Yes, I gave another party the next week, and I froze two freezers of ice cream. And I invited every Jack one of those fellows who committed that "*dastardly deed*—and do you know, strange as it might appear, every one of the culprits was there. First one started to boohoo and then another and before the party was over every boy put his hand in mine and asked forgiveness. Bishop, those fellows today are some of the best citizens in this town."

Folks, that man was wise. He rubbed them the right way at a critical time. Like old Dave Harum, it was a kind hand on their heads that shaped their lives. *Don't give a boy a bad start.*

STORY THIRTEEN

"Put it into them when they're young and take it out vhen they're old" is nothing more than putting the words of the scriptures in another way. I refer to, "Train up a child in the way he should go, and when he is old he will not depart therefrom." Mr. Father and dear Mother, don't kid yourselves. If you are going to have men or women of real integrity, you have got to put it into them when they are young. If you don't, you will never take it out when they're old.

The above picture is suggested to the writer by a story told by Bishop LeGrand Richards a year or so ago. I am giving him credit for the story and I think it one of the most bracing and humorous stories I have ever heard. Here is the story:—

A country boy was being visited by his city cousin. As the latter did his regular chores the city boy followed him about. Of course the city boy was curious about some of the things included in these chores. The country boy's life was so different. I don't suppose the city lad knew too much about where milk came from except that they found it on the doorstep each morning. Well, this particular night the city boy followed the country cousin about while he did his chores. The farm boy took two buckets from the kitchen, one full of milk and the other empty. With the two buckets in hand he moved down towards the corral. Something in the corral smelled the milk in the bucket, started to cut capers in the corral, and by the time the two boys arrived the calf was waiting hysterically for the contents of one of the buckets. The country cousin braced the bucket well with his feet, and in a very few minutes the calf had devoured the bucket of milk. The boy then took the empty bucket and proceeded to the corner of the corral where the cow was innocently chewing her cud. The country boy sat down and proceeded to milk the cow. The boy from the city was looking on in wonderment at these new experiences, the calf devouring the milk in a hurry and seeing his cousin proceed to pump the cow for the milk. The city boy stepped back, scratched his head, and then with delight exclaimed, "*I see, you put it into them when they're young and take it out when they're old.*"

Lincoln's greatness was put into him when he was young. On the school grounds when he was about ten years of age, his playmates had found a turtle in the ditch and had proceeded to take the hot coals from the school and place them on the turtle's back to see him wiggle. Immediately our champion rolled up his sleeves and shaking his fists at his young comrades defied them with this statement:— "You try that again, and you'll answer to these" (speaking of his fists).

The great Emancipation act was nothing more than the crystallization of the teachings of his mother that prompted "you try that again and you'll answer to these." At eighteen, while at New Orleans, when he saw a black man to be auctioned as a common critter he vehemently observed, "If I ever get chance to hit that, I will hit it hard."

When you stand next time at the side of a steaming locomotive with the Herculean power to draw one hundred and fifty cars laden with tanks over the hills, please think of a sickly little fellow at home with nothing else to do but throttle the throat of a steaming tea kettle to see it explode its lid. You have to think of James Watt, the inventor of the first steam engine. The seed was there as a boy, and afterwards developed into the man inventor.

The steamboat was invented by Fulton. The fundamentals of that new invention were put into action by young Fulton as a boy fishing, not with an oar on each side of the boat, but a little paddle operated from a crank from inside the boat.

Ulysses S. Grant, the man who brought the Civil War to a close, at twelve would go to the mountains, drag on the logs, bind them with chains, and deliver the wood home without help of an adult.

Edison, who gave you the incandescent light and a hundred other inventions, as a lad was found in the middle of the night when his folks were asleep electrocuting cockroaches on the kitchen floor.

Florence Nightingale, "The lady with a lamp," was probably one of the most popular women that ever graced the world. Her nursing started as a little girl in helping a lame dog she found on the road from school. Someone instilled in her heart a seed that afterwards developed into the great nurse of the Crimean and other wars.

Teach a child in its youth to be kind to the aged, and you will find that child gracious to others in its maturity. Spoil a child; let it be selfish, and, when it is over twenty-one, that's the kind of a person you will have. If you are going to take it out when they're old, you've got to put it into them when they're young.

STORY FOURTEEN

BISHOP: ARE YOU USING YOUR YOUNG PEOPLE?

Someone has wisely said, "Youth for action, age for wisdom." This is very true, and it is also true that there is no substitute for experience, but you will not function one hundred percent unless you call into your councils the young people. Have your ear to the ground and be sure you hear distinctly the patter of their feet. Don't forget what youth has done for the world. We need the inspiration of the red corpuscles of their blood. Invite them into your councils. If you want to get into a rut, keep away from close contact with your boys and girls. "The only difference between a rut and a grave is that one is deeper than the other." Have the youth at your elbows when you do your planning, and let them help execute the plans with you. The problems of the youth have probably never been so great as they are today. If ever they needed the hand of older people on their shoulders to guide them, it is now. One of the wisest things said by the Prophet was, in effect, "Teach people right principles and let them govern themselves." And don't forget for a minute that this philosophy applies to youth. Bishop, let them govern themselves. Let them feel they are directors in your ward corporation. The corporation needs the vision and, if you please, the vitality and spunk of the youth. Let us, who are not so young as we used to be, and we mean emphatically those of us holding positions of presidency and leadership in this Church, keep the youth close to us. The young need the experience of the older folks, but, we equally need the vision and viewpoint of our children.

Please keep in mind, bishop, that one of your major responsibilities is the youth. It is largely true that if you take care of the youth, you take care of all.

Lest there be some who haven't heard the following story—may we repeat it. It so well clinches this philosophy, we'll risk being on the side of triteness in hope clarity will overcome it. This story has been very aptly used by Bishop Richards:

The father wants to read the newspaper, but he is disturbed by his inquisitive son who is demanding his attention. The father has a bright idea and decides to occupy the boy's attention another way. He rips from a magazine a page on which is a map of the world. Thinks he, "I'll make a jig-saw puzzle of the map of the world and while this lad is laboriously putting it together, I'll have an hour of peaceful bliss reading the news." A pair of scissors is brought into play and the page is cut into a hundred pieces. The boy sets to work, but the good dad has only five minutes of peace! The map of the world is all together again—every piece of it in its place. But what happened? How could he finish the task so quickly? The boy's answer was enough, "You see, Dad, on the other side of the page where the map was, was a picture of a boy. I put the boy together, and the world took care of itself." If we would take care of the boy, the world would be all right.

A good portion of the mistakes of adults are traceable to misguided youth, and half of the misguiding is because we who represent the leadership of the Church forget what we used to be and what we used to like to do. Let's get close to youth and feel their pulse. Yes, let them help shape their own destiny. Let them in on our councils. Whether we are dads or mothers, leaders, or associated in some way with the young people, let them in on our councils.

STORY FIFTEEN

> The boast of heraldry, the pomp of pow'r,
> And all that beauty, all that wealth e'er gave,
> Awaits alike thy inevitable hour,
> The paths of glory lead but to the grave.

These words are taken from Gray's "Elegy" and were read by General Wolfe to his men as they stealthily paddled down the St. Lawrence River the night before he and his brave fellows captured Quebec from the French. After he had read the poem, he turned to his men and said something like this: "I would rather be the author of that poem than conquer Quebec tomorrow."

He did take the Gibraltar of America, but both the great General Montcalm and Wolfe himself bit the earth next day reminding all of us again of the fact that pomp of power, wealth, and all that glitters with fame await the inevitable hour when the path of each leads to the tombstone.

Someone has said that men on the board of life are like men you play with in the game of chess. In the course of the game some are crowned, some are given other scepters of power, but when the game is over all the players on the stage in the game are put back into the box together.

General Wolfe was only twenty-six years old when he charged Montcalm's forces. He was engaged to a beautiful girl in England, and their plans contemplated all that happiness could mean, but he was laid low.

In this old world with its sunshine and happiness we must be prepared for clouds and sorrows, yes, the shocks. Yes, we must be ready for what happens. The more we are prepared the less will be the shock.

> When death puts out the flame, the snuff will tell
> If you're wax or tallow, by the smell.

The above was from the pen of Benjamin Franklin, one of the wisest philosophers of American history. On reading it, it may sound a little crude, but there is a deep-seated common sense that gets hold of you.

As dear old Saint Paul put it, "If in this life only we have hope in Christ, we are of all men most miserable." Yes, in the proper value of things we must "hitch our wagon to a star." Are your contemplations hitched to things of this world or is there something over the horizon that beckons you on?

In the midst of the last war a doctor on leave and attending a Church service was called upon to express himself. Among the inspiring words he uttered were the following:—"The

Lord must have known there was something very interesting over the horizon or he wouldn't have permitted his prophet's life to be taken by a mob at Carthage. The Creator of all of us had in mind the glories over the rainbow or he wouldn't have permitted the rabble to hang on a cross his only Begotten Son. Brothers and Sisters, as I fly from the battlefield to the hospitals with our brave fellows, I try to take an attitude like this:—'Lord, if you want me today, I'm ready.' "

Some months ago the observations of a mother of two sons in the war came to me. Said she to a friend, "If anything happens to either one of my boys, I don't know whether the gospel is true or not."

Dear reader, I ask you this question, "Is the gospel true as long as God doesn't let death visit your abode, and not to be believed if the Reaper knocks at our door?" In other words, when you are put to the test, are you "wax" or "tallow?" What does the reaction or the smell indicate when "death puts out the flame?" In other words, can you take it on the chin and keep your equilibrium? Do you think hard enough when you see the inroads made into the homes of your friends from time to time to realize that your threshold, too, will be darkened by the shadow of death?

Whoever did this deep-set thinking was a real philosopher. "If you expect death as a friend, prepare to entertain it. If you expect death as an enemy, prepare to overcome it. Death has no advantage unless it comes as a stranger."

If you are a sinner, change your life that you might entertain death as a friend. If you are consistent in your life, you are prepared to say to him what the young lieutenant said flying over the land, "Lord, if you want me today, I am ready."

One of the most beautiful stories I have ever read was told in the Scout manual many years ago. Of course the story was told to clinch the Scout philosophy "Be prepared." Will you let me tell the story?

Many years ago the old country fair in parts of England was, besides being the place of exhibition for farm products, where employer and employee met. A farmer here sought his help for the coming year, and young and old went to the fair to be employed.

Farmer Smith wanted a boy to work on his farm. He was doing some interviewing of candidates. A thoughtful looking lad of about sixteen attracted him. The boy was confronted with a rather abrupt question from the gruff old agriculturist. "What can you do?" The boy swung back at him in the same style, "I can sleep when the wind blows."

It was no wonder at all that the farmer turned right-about-face to others for the help he needed on receiving such an answer. Notwithstanding he didn't particularly like the answer to a civil question he got from the teen-ager, there was something about the gray eyes of that fellow that got under his skin.

He approached the lad again with the same question, "What did you say you could do?" Again the same answer bounced back at him, "I can sleep when the wind blows."

Mr. Smith was still disgusted with such an answer and went to other parts of the fair to look into the faces of other youngsters who might want a job on a farm, but there was something about that answer he got that stuck to him like glue. First thing he knew his feet were carrying him back to meet the steady gaze of those deliberate eyes of the boy with such strange language.

"What did you say you could do?" for the third time he

thundered at the farm help. For the third time, too, the farmer got the same answer: "I can sleep when the wind blows."

"Get into the wagon—we'll try you out."

Now, according to the story, we don't hear very much about our boy and how he was getting along with his new employer for several weeks, but we can guess pretty accurately that his time had been occupied pretty well.

One night Farmer Smith was waked about 2:00 a.m. with what might be a cyclone. It seemed that gusts from the north in only a few minutes developed with intensity to threaten the roof over his head. The trees cracked and noises outside turned the nervous system of our friend upside down. The speed he used to jump into his trousers was only outdone by the lightning as it broke up the darkness outside. With shoes half-laced he rushed out into the farmyard to see if anything on the premises was still intact, but he would need the services on a wicked night like this of that new boy. He called up the stairs of the attic where the latter slept, but the response was the healthy lung heaving of a healthy lad. He went half the way up the stairs and thundered again, but only a snore echoed back. In excitement he went to the boy's bed and did everything but tear the bed clothes from the youth, but the lad slept on.

With a mixture of desperation and disgust he faced the gale, and out into the farmyard he plunged. He first approached the cow barn. Lo and behold, the milk producers were peacefully chewing their cuds, and the inside of their abode was as snug as a mouse under a haystack. It didn't take him long to discover how the boy had chinked up the cracks of the cow abode and re-establish the locks and hinges. In the pigpen he found the same tranquility, notwithstanding the forces at work that night.

He turned to the haystack. As he felt about in the darkness, it didn't take him very long to determine again the preparation of the lad with the gray, steady eyes. Every few feet on that feed stack wires had been thrown and weighted on each side. With this construction the alfalfa was peacefully under control and laughing at the elements.

Our farmer friend was stunned with what revelations he had in a few minutes on that night of the cyclone. He dropped his head. His mental maneuvers shot like lightning to the boy snoring in the attic. Again, the peculiar answer of a few weeks ago slapped him in the face: "I can sleep when the wind blows."

Dear reader, can you sleep when the wind blows? Just as sure as your heart is ticking, there will be a night in your life when there will be a cyclone overhead. Sooner or later it sweeps over every home. Are you prepared? Have you prepared yourself for that night when it comes? Have you developed your faith so that the cracks of despair are eliminated and you have a philosophy that will withstand the blasts? Have you built so that your structures can stand the bolts from the sky? Have you put wires every few feet and weighted them on the ends?

Can you stand erect and under full control say to your Creator, "Lord, if you want me today, I'm ready"? When death puts out the flame, does the atmosphere indicate you are wax or tallow?

"If you expect death as a friend, be prepared to entertain him."

I will never forget the impression the story below made on me which was told to me by my mother.

Tender-handed stroke a nettle,
And it stings you for your pains;
Grasp it like a man of mettle,
And it soft as silk remains.

STORY SIXTEEN

IN WHICH PLACE ARE YOUR YOUNG PEOPLE?

Bishop, in which place are your young people? Don't forget, bishop, that your young people are just as full of human nature as you were at their age, and don't forget they crave pleasure just as much as the young folks anywhere else. Old Dave Harum used to say, "There's as much human nature in some of us as there is in others, if not more." Now, bishop, that young generation in your ward is going to be found in one of these two places. If your community is not providing wholesome amusement for these folk, they are going to seek it in a "dive." Don't kid yourself. Bishop, did you ever visit one of these latter places? Take your wife with you some night and drop in and see what's going on. If you are afraid that you will be talked about because of being seen in such a place, get an officer of the law to accompany you. See for yourself what temptation is here. See for yourself that men who run these places are more concerned in the dollar's profit than they are in the virtue of a boy or girl. Someone has wisely said, "If you must, bring merriment to the churches, for the devil will furnish it in hell." In plain American English, if your young people are going to these roadhouses because dances and such amusement are not furnished in your community, you have something for which you must answer.

Did you ever figure what part amusements play in the shaping of our destinies? It's probably true that it is through the contacts we make in our amusements, that many of us pick our partners for life. Some fellow who knew what he was talking about on this subject said, "Education is a good deal like eating; a fellow can't always tell which particular thing did him good, but he can usually tell which did him harm. It's down among the sweets, among his amusements and recreations that he's going to find his stomach-ache." Bishop, it's down in their sweets that we want to guide them. Are you close to the youth? Do they feel free enough with you that they will tell you their problems? Is there a chasm between you and them? If there is, put a bridge over it quickly. You are probably old enough to be a father to most of them, but remember, attitude is what makes you old or young.

Great events in history are the result of little things. Printing came to the world because one John Gutenberg accidentally dropped into a kettle of dye a wooden letter cut almost absent-mindedly from a tree, with a jackknife. We almost stumbled onto the law of gravity because an apple thumped to the ground under the eyes of observing Newton.

An innocent visit of Eli Whitney to a southern home resulted in the cotton gin and a revolution in the cotton industry. Yes, a flock of birds flying over the bow of Christopher Columbus' ship shaped the destiny of America.

And you may go on and on.

Yes, lives are made successful or they are ruined by a twist of our wrists. A little planning on our part determines great events in the lives of our young people.

Bishop, plan for your young people. They never needed your kindness and fatherly guidance more than now. This war has given them problems that you and the rest of us haven't had. This war is making difficult problems for them in their love affairs. If ever we should be at our wits' ends in cooperating with them, it is now. Get the people of your ward to get this vision of things. It will cost something, surely, but where better can we invest our dollars than in the lives of the finest people in the world? What does it profit us if we have a thousand cattle on a thousand hills and because of our false economy our young people are in "dives" and "joints"?

STORY SEVENTEEN

BY THE GRAPEVINE WAY

John Barleycorn is not the only cause of some of the saddest things on mother earth. Much comes from the grape. If we would confine our use of it to eating the grape itself or to drinking the juice thereof when it's fresh, all would be well in the world, but we don't. We squeeze the juice out and let it stand and work its head off. Then we drink it, and then we get "fresh."

Cheney in his wonderful book, *Stories for Talks to Boys,* tells a wonderful story. Let me tell it to you. The illustration of it is drawn on the preceding page:—

When they planted the first grapevine they killed a peacock and sprinkled its blood so that the roots of this popular plant would absorb it. When the plant started to stick its nose out of the ground, they killed another animal and spread its blood so it would lend itself to the growth of the grape. This animal was the monkey. The vine has now started to grow with vigor. They killed a third animal, and this is the king of beasts, the lion.

Now, to finish the job! When the grape is just about ready to bring forth its fruit, they kill a pig.

Well, we're talking in parables, aren't we? Let's get down to tacks:—When a boy takes one glass, he's inclined to strut as proudly as a peacock. He takes a second or a third glass and then makes a monkey of himself. Continuing with his drinking his face reddens, and he roars like a lion. Yes, he can lick anything in the country. (However, he may have the same experience that a little Irishman had who, having indulged similarly, said he could lick anything in the country. After he came to, after some fellow close by had heard his challenge and had lifted him under the chin, he calmly exclaimed, "I guess I took in too much territory.") Well, to continue our story, if he continues to drink of the fermented wine juice, he finally rolls in the gutter like a pig.

This isn't fiction. It's real life. Just keep your eyes half open and see the scenes from life just like this. You don't have to read newspapers or books. These experiences come under your nose every day. Let me give you a little experience I had not too many moons away:—

A lady of about thirty-five years of age was ushered into my office. She asked if she might talk to me privately. I closed all the doors, and she unburdened her soul to me. Of course, she didn't want anyone to hear her story. She was naturally a very good-looking woman, but this day her cheek-bones were high, and her face was drawn down with unusual anxiety and worry. She asked me if I would go up to the state prison the coming Saturday at 1:00 p.m. Just what was her trouble? Her husband was behind bars, and his hearing before the Governor and the Board of Pardons would be heard the date mentioned above. She wanted him out by June 1 (If I might be so frank with you, she was going through the valley of death the third time, and she wanted the father of the child to be born to hold her hand in the coming ordeal.) By the way, I consented to do all I could for her husband.

That Saturday the reception room of the penitentiary was crowded, and people interested in this particular fellow were standing around the steps. You inquire, "What was he in there for?" I'll tell you, and, by the way, that man in that jail was one of the finest mechanics in Salt Lake City.

It was a Saturday night party, and they were determined to have a good time. To make the crowd merry—to help out conversation, etc., etc., they brought some of that stuff we are talking about into the party. The subject of our story took a couple of drinks and acted as proud as a peacock. He drank a couple more and then made a monkey of himself. After drinking a couple more, and like our story, he roared like a lion. In this heated moment he grabbed a butcher knife close by his hands, threw it across the room, taking off, if you please, part of the face of a lady who was a near relative.

The state had to make an example of such conduct, and the husband of that splendid woman, and the father of those beautiful girls was in a cell like other criminals.

Yes, may I tell you he didn't get out by June 1, and I

don't need to tell you that good woman and her family are still living down the fact that her husband and their father was a "jailbird." Unless the family move to remote parts, they never can live it down. And we may add, if he doesn't watch his step, he'll crawl in the gutter like a pig.

How much would that father give to take out of his life that one night of bad judgment and foolishness? But it's done. Remorse won't take away the result of the night they had to bring that stuff into the home to make the crowd merry. That father got his eyes open, it's true, but a little too late.

That reminds me of the little Negro who fell in love with a little black and white kitten belonging to his neighbor. The kitten was just two days old, but the little black fellow insisted that he wanted that black and white kitten for his own. His good neighbor insisted that the little creature would die if it wasn't left with its mother for two or three weeks at least. But the lad wasn't satisfied. He wanted the idol of his eye right that day, and he acted accordingly.

When the shades of night had begun to fall, with match in hand he stealthily crept over to his neighbor's. He located the shed where the old cat had her brood, lit a match, found the cracked box wherein were deposited the young family of kittens. With the help of a second match he identified black and white kitten, tucked it under his coat and ran hurriedly to his home. He wrapped the little creature snugly into an old coat, did everything but kiss it goodnight, and went to bed.

All during the night visions of his new prize danced in his head. Just at daybreak he hastened down to the basement to see how the kitten had fared during the night.

Lo and behold, during the night it had kicked off its bed clothes and had subjected itself to the consequences of the chill of the night. Of course, it was just too much resistance for the tiny body to overcome, and it lay stiff as a poker with its eyes wide open. The little fellow with tears doing everything they could to clean his face looked down at the motionless pride of his heart and moaned out, "Ain't it funny, now yo's dead yo got your eyes open."

Yes, people who monkey with that stuff get their eyes opened after it is too late.

Some months ago a dear friend of mine called me on the telephone and pleaded with me to go to the penitentiary to intercede with the Board of Pardons to get his son out of jail. What was he there for? He had a few drinks and while crossing Main and Second South that morning all he did was to kill an innocent pedestrian in the way of the car driven by a drunken driver. Remorse—is it there? Yes, but like the kitten, now he is dead he has his eyes open.

Last May a young Mexican graduate from the Juarez Academy came to be interviewed for a mission. He told me the following story:- His father was a habitual drinker. Whenever he got drunk, it meant a whipping for his mother. One day his father came home drunk and said to his wife:- "Mary, when I don't come home this way you will be happy, won't you?" "Yes, George, I will." He pulled a six-shooter out of his pocket, shot his wife, the mother of this boy, through the head and then killed himself. As luck happened, the bullet aimed at the boy's mother hit the optic nerve, and the only permanent injury she received was the loss of the sight in one of her eyes. He was like the lion—"When the stars come out tonight, he is under six feet of ground."

I was visiting a stake in northern Idaho just a couple of months ago and heard this tragic story:- The father came home intoxicated, pulled a six-shooter, aimed at his wife, missed her, and killed his eight-year-old daughter. Last Christmas another intoxicated father came home, started beating his wife. A young lad about fourteen, to protect his mother, pulled out a gun and laid low his father, and again, "When the stars come out tonight another man is under six feet of ground." He, too, roared like a lion under the influence of drink.

> Humpty Dumpty sat on a wall,
> Humpty Dumpty had a great fall;
> All the king's horses and all the king's men
> Couldn't put Humpty Dumpty together again.

You can't call those men back to life. The trail is just as definite as it can be. First, we are proud as peacocks. Second, we make monkeys out of ourselves. Third, we roar like lions; we stop at nothing. Finally, we roll in the gutter like pigs.

STORY EIGHTEEN

ALL THAT COUNTS IS THE SHINE

Sometime ago in a committee meeting, President Clark told the following story. It is illustrated in the cartoon.

With a friend, he stepped into a bootblack parlor for a shine. Two colored bootblacks began immediately to work on the two pair of shoes. The boy working on President Clark's shoes was very methodical and proceeded to do his job accordingly. Every stroke counted, but there were no frills. The other bootblack was working with much more pomp and show. He would snap the rag, beat a tattoo with it, and do everything but play a jazz tune. The friend said to the bootblack shining President Clark's shoes, "Why do you not use all these frills and flourishes on my friend's shoes? He's not getting his money's worth." The bootblack shining President Clark's shoes looked up at the friend and pointing to the boy, evidently a newcomer, shining the friend's shoes, said: "When he's been here as long as I have, he'll know that nuthin' counts but the shine."

That story doesn't get away from me. I often think of it and its application. I used to work with brick masons and carpenters. The man who accomplished the most and was the most efficient brick layer wasn't the man noted for flourishes of his trowel and false motions; he was the man who could put the most bricks in the wall and have them laid true and uniform. The best carpenter was not the man who made a lot of flourishes with his hammer and saw—it was the man who cut the boards the most rapidly and put them in place in the quickest workmanlike way. It is true of the stonecutter and the lawyer. It is the lawyer who wins cases whom one wants to take care of his legal business. One doesn't estimate the value of a schoolteacher by how loudly she talks and how many motions she goes through, but how many boys and girls she prepares and trains for real life.

If we are not careful in our Church activities and responsibilities, we are apt to measure a man or a woman by the flourishes he makes and his false motions. What really counts is what is accomplished. The only thing that counts is the results. The proof of the pudding is in the eating.

Ofttimes, we have to observe ourselves from a distance to get the proper viewpoint of our responsibilities and how well we are meeting them. Sometimes it is good to stop, look, and listen, or as someone has said, to stand off and see ourselves go by. An artist couldn't create a masterpiece if he didn't continually stand off from his painting to get the proper perspective. We have to ask ourselves eternally, "What am I trying to accomplish? What is it all about? What really counts?" *All that counts is the shine.* A customer is not interested in how many times the boy can throw the rag around his head and snap it like a whip. All he is interested in is that when he leaves the bootblack parlor his shoes have been shined properly.

I have mentioned the following illustration before. Pardon my using it again. The most successful fishing in the Hawaiian Islands is accomplished by the fishermen whose activities are directed by a companion on top of the hill overlooking the waters. The fisherman proper is too close to the fish to see them, but because the other is high above the water he can see the runs of the fish and can direct the fishermen where to put their nets. I repeat, we have to get away from ourselves to appreciate in the best way what our aims are.

Like the bootblack we, in our Church work, ofttimes make many false motions. We forget what we are aiming to do. The goal of the Relief Society workers should be singly and collectively to raise the standards of the people of the group or ward in which they are working. The question to ask themselves is, "How many lives and families have we benefited?" Primarily, that is what counts. The Primary teacher should have as her aim, "Into how many little children can I put the spirit of the gospel and prepare them to appreciate the contacts they will make later in other organizations of the Church?" Her question will be, "How am I influencing these boys and girls intellectually and spiritually?" Any motions she goes through which do not result in these accomplishments are lost. It is the same with Sunday School and M.I.A. workers. You ward teachers, how many calls you make per month, how near you hit the one hundred percent mark of visits each month, is not nearly so important as how you are influencing the people on whom you call. Again I repeat, it isn't the motions you go through; rather, it is how well you get in gear in your responsibilities and aims.

In many of our activities, our engines are racing and going much faster than the wheels are turning, because we forget that *all that counts is the shine*.

Ward bishops, are you burning up your engine? Are you going through a lot of false motions? Do you pride yourself on how many nights a week you are working? *Stop, look and listen,* and study carefully what movements count, and what false motions you may omit. Many a bishop who is burning up his engine, if he would stop, look, and listen, and study his movements, could be more efficient.

We all take our hats off to the man who is diligent in the duties of the ward or stake, but much more could be accomplished in this Church if we would move more slowly and study our motions more carefully. In other words, if we would pour into our souls this philosophy mentioned by President Clark, that *all that counts is the shine,* we would do much better work, live longer, and our families would be happier living with us.

Christ influenced the world by simplicity.

STORY NINETEEN

OUR PRAYERS SHOULD BE SIMPLE

"And when thou prayest, thou shalt not be as the hypocrites are: for they love to pray standing in the synagogues and in the corners of the streets, that they may be seen of men. Verily I say unto you, They have their reward.

"But thou, when thou prayest, enter into thy closet, and when thou hast shut thy door, pray to thy Father which is in secret; and thy Father which seeth in secret shall reward thee openly.

"But when ye pray, use not vain repetitions, as the heathen do: for they think that they shall be heard for their much speaking." (Matt. 6:5-7.)

The advice given above came from the Master nearly two thousand years ago, but we still need it. The Lord's prayer is wonderful because of its simplicity. We still have people who have the notion that a long prayer will make up for other deficiencies. The ancient Pharisees were not the only ones that needed that medicine. It applies today. Prayer alone won't get us to first base in regions above. "Not everyone that sayeth 'Lord, Lord' shall enter the kingdom of heaven, but he that doeth the will of our Father which is in heaven." (Matt. 7:21.)

We ought to let that advice sink in. Some of us ought to have it burned into our hides with a branding iron. The trouble with a lot of us is that we think such advice always belongs to the old Pharisees. Someone has said, "Duty is something disagreeable that the other fellow ought to do." Yes, "charity begins at home."

I often think of the old fellow down our way who used to get up on fast days and say, "I just can't rest until I have borne my testimony." The trouble with him was that he bore his testimony the first part of the meeting and then went sound asleep and pretty nearly snored his head off. Now are you doing that? Am I doing it? It is one thing to have a testimony and another thing to do something about it. Don't you think that I have so little sense that I am speaking disparagingly of the testimony of a humble person. The Church rests on that kind of faith. My mother taught me at her knee just how important that is.

To illustrate what I am driving at, may I tell a story that was told to us down in Lehi at a recent conference there. A good patriarch said that he was asked to take his saw and hammer, but he couldn't find the saw. He hunted all over for it, and finally his wife came to the rescue. She said, "Now, Father, if I were you I would think where I used that saw last, and I believe I would hunt in that place." Well, he went everywhere in search of the saw. He looked high and low ever trying to think where he last used the saw and praying that he might be guided to the lost article. He climbed on the roof—no saw in sight. At that moment, when he was about to despair, although it was a breezeless day, a slight stir of the air tipped the saw from the top of the chimney. It whirled through the air and stuck in the shingled roof a few feet ahead of him like the alighting of an arrow. In soliloquizing about its almost miraculous restoration, our patriarch remarked to us, "I thought I saw the hand of the Lord in that saw. But," emphasized he, "I was dead sure the Lord wanted me to see the hand of the saw." Now, it is easier to see the hand of the Lord in things than it is to see the hand of the saw.

Someone has wisely said, "Many a man has made a false step by standing still." A good member of our Church who is more skilful in the use of the baton than he is in penmanship stated that in giving the name of a hymn to be sung as, "Sweet and Low," the brother presiding announced it as, "Sweat and Sow." Rather an odd coincidence, but life is more "sweat and sow" than it is "sweet and low."

Prayer is pretty sacred business to talk about, but many a man has made it anything but sacred in stretching it out. Many stories have been told of the length of some prayers, and how, it is sad to say, they have been made light of. I guess in some circles they have been so long that they went against the grain of many a red-blooded American lad, and I suppose sometimes things were done by the boys that didn't breathe reverence. I have heard of a father whose prayer covered so much territory that the boys could get up from their knees, have an inning of baseball and return only to find the prayer, as the boy put it, "just down to the ten tribes." Of course, that's ridiculous, but nevertheless, such a prayer suggested anything but supplication. In that home prayer was overdone. Yes, in that home there would have been more devotion if there had been shorter prayers by virtue of each member of the family taking his turn.

To illustrate what I am driving at, let me tell you the story of sanctimonious Deacon Jones. He'd skin a flea for its hide; you'd have to hold on fast to your purse in a trade or business venture; but in his prayers he was both pious and long-winded.

He was a sanctimonious, wonderful fellow on the Sabbath day, but during the week you had to hold on tight to your eyebrows or he would take them, too,—one of those two-faced "angelic" souls that grace this world; the kind Christ speaks of in his rebuke to the old Pharisees; a front as pious as apple sauce, but a rail on the sands of time of dead men's bones. He was on his deathbed; he was doomed to go. He had made quite an impression on some of the village who did not think very straight; but he did not fool the boys. The boys had his number. He began to sink and sink, and finally he got so low that instead of answering the doorbell or the knock on the door by the inquirers, they had a blackboard put out in front of his abode. Every half hour the attending physician gave his temperature and his pulse. There was quite a commotion in the village; everybody was watching that blackboard. Well, the boys watched it, too, and they were waiting for an opportunity to express themselves. (If you ever want to get the proper value on yourself, ask the boys.) I think the last bulletin read, "8:05 a. m.—pulse, 50, temperature 86." When nobody was looking, a bright lad, with mischief bent, who knew the Deacon, slipped up with a piece of chalk, and excitingly recorded: "8:22¼ a. m. Much excitement in hell; Deacon Jones not yet arrived."

Too long prayers in home and in Church have taken their toll. Many a boy has been riven from sanctity and worship by continual overdoses of longevity in prayers. A father in his home with a family who prays ten to twenty minutes has something to answer for. I am sure many a good lad has rebelled against such "vain repetitions." Instead of pulling a boy to wholesome devotion, he has "rebelled against it."

I like to hear a prayer sincere but well put together. We owe it to one another when one of us prays for the group, that the prayer be logical, to the point, and run smoothly, but above all it should be from the heart. It should be simple. If we would take twenty-three hours out of the twenty-four each day to remind the Lord how grateful we are for our different blessings and enumerate the different things, we never could have enough time to do it. "For your Father knoweth what things ye have need of, before ye ask."

Very often when a man is called to the pulpit to open or close a meeting, the length of his prayer would indicate the fellow was afraid he wouldn't be called before the public for another ten years and was going to take advantage of this particular opportunity to discourse. I like a short prayer, and I believe my tastes along this line are like those of most people. I like a short letter, don't you? I don't have much idea as to the organization on high in recording and listening to the prayers directed there, but I imagine sometimes even the recording angels up there whisper to one another accordingly, "oh how I wish that fellow's prayers were shorter."

STORY TWENTY

Mr. Church Officer, do you *swell* with your job or do you *grow* with it? Do you consider your job as a *position* or an *opportunity* no matter what your devotions or ambitions may be, probably no greater opportunity could come your way, under which to grow, than in the office that is yours. Yes, there are blessings that come with your responsibility, but if you are to have those blessings, you've got to go out and get them. We are not forgetting virtues you must have. We are not forgetting charity and all that this word means; we are not forgetting prayer. If you are not prayerful, you will go flat in your responsibilities. But, we repeat, you must *grow* in your position. Some people *swell* in a position instead.

Someone has said, "Thou shalt not take thyself too seriously." Let's take our job seriously, but not *ourselves*. Robert Burns said, "O wad some power the giftie gie us to see oursel's as ithers see us! It wad frae monie a blunder free us." Someone else having in mind a self-centered individual's conception of himself has aptly changed the above wording to read: "Oh, wad some power to others gie. To see myself as I see me."

To your people, are you a progressive, on-your-toes servant, or do they see you *smug* in the glories of your authority? Mr. Officer, are you learning more about your job every day and functioning the most modern way? Are you content to do things as those things were done fifty years ago or do you know the short cuts? Are you alert, searching for new ideas and new methods? "The Lord feeds the birds, but He doesn't take the worms to their nests." Lorimer, who wrote the book, *Letters of a Self-made Merchant to His Son,* says, "You can still kill ducks with a muzzle-loader, but if you want to take as many ducks home as the other fellow, you've got to carry a hammerless." Since he wrote those words, even the hammerless is old-fashioned. Now you've got to carry an automatic. "As with the priest, so with the people." That saying is almost as old as the hills, but it is true. Are you a light to the people of your organization or are they behind the times because of your lack of vision?

Sometime ago at a farm convention, an implement salesman was explaining a new twelve-inch plow, said plow to be used in the spring to scrape the accumulated moss from the irrigation ditches. The sales talk went over very well, and the farmers were very much interested. In the salesman's invitation for questions one wide-awake young farmer from a "Sleepy Hollow" village raised his hand and asked, "Mr. Johnson, your company, I suppose, wouldn't make a plow of that design, the blade being about two inches, would it?" Of course, the salesman was as inquisitive as he was interested in the question. "My dear friend," asked he, "to what use would you want to put a blade only two inches wide?" Then came the answer, "Mr. Johnson, we have just a lot of old mossbacks over in our section, and if we had a two-inch blade of this kind to run up and down their backs, it would be a wonderful thing for the community." Are we mossbacks? Are we *alive?*

If there ever was a time of adjustment it is *now*. If you can't conform yourself to new changes, you are going to find yourself "out on a limb." Those who have eyes and see not, and those with ears who hear not are in for trouble. There are those who pretend to play the roll of leadership, who are uncomfortable in confronting new ideas and new methods. You can bet your life, ahead of us it is going to be the survival of the fittest. He who cannot adjust himself is going to be left behind.

They tell a story of a fellow who with others was running a race, the race to end after the runners had gone around the track several times. They had been going around a few times, and the finishing lap was getting close. Sitting close to his good dad, a wide-awake lad, keyed up to see the finish of the race, observing a particular contestant losing ground, said, "*Look, Dad, that guy is so far behind that he thinks he is on ahead!*"

Mr. Church Leader, do you get into that embarrassing position where you are so far behind that you think you are ahead? Do you *swell* or *grow* with your Church responsibilities?

STORY TWENTY-ONE

Bishop, don't forget the bone and sinew of this Church lies in the common people. The sacrifice made by the meek and lowly has kept this Church rolling. That deep-seated faith, a synonym of "I'll do or die," is the Mormon philosophy which has weathered the storms of a hundred years.

This little meek and lowly soul in our picture is the particular type I have in mind. They are not the flowers that "blush unseen and waste their fragrance on the desert air." She represents the quiet, deep-seated force that has startled the world. Notice how modestly she slips into the box her contribution. What she is doing today as a gift is only a shadow of what she is doing in other directions about which only she and the Lord, and maybe a few close relatives or friends, know anything.

A few days ago while attending a stake conference in one of our rural districts, as I ascended the steps to the tabernacle, I was rather impressed with the carriage and demeanor of an unpretentious, dear lady of probably seventy-five years of age. You know, some faces and attitudes of people, no matter how lowly they walk, just impress you. This lady impressed me. For some reason as I approached her, my hand automatically went to her arm to help her up the stairway. When we arrived at the assembly room and I had been introduced to the good lady about whom we are speaking, the president of the stake with whom I had approached the tabernacle stopped me and said, "Do you know whom you have helped up those steps?" And he told me. "That little woman has raised eight of her own children and eight others, the children of a former wife of her faithful husband." Yes, she had been a mother to sixteen children. Practically all, if not all of those sons of that family had been sent to college and on missions. A humble eighty acres of well-tilled land before depressions, during depressions, and after depressions, had kept that family intact, had fed that family, given them a liberal education, and had them do their duty to their Church. While other families drove their limousines, this family, when times got the toughest, rode to and from market in a horse-drawn vehicle, kept their bills paid, and made their donations in cash and man-power to their religion. But don't forget, it requires a self-sacrificing woman teamed with a God-fearing husband to accomplish these things.

Bishop, don't forget the widow's mite. There's a force, a potentiality there that doesn't parade itself. Like floating ice encountered in the deep seas—don't forget, you see only a fraction of the real thing. Seven-eighths of it is a driving force you don't see on the surface.

Thank the Lord we don't have many pharisaical individuals in our Church like the one in his dress suit shown in our picture at the beginning of this chapter. Yes, let us be happy we have a few who do things to be seen of men. We appreciate in our Church the large donations given to the Church by those who are able. Those large contributions help us do things we could never do without them. And don't forget we do some mighty big things because of these generous people, but the virtue is not in the size of the gift but in the sacrifice made. The world will never know how many women take in washing to keep a son or husband in the mission field.

Another woman met the breakers of storm like a veteran captain meets the blasts of the mighty deep.

After one of these blasts swept from the family deck her breadwinner and patriarch, she met the crisis with chin up and a defiance that only a Mormon mother can have. She didn't sit down to weep or to pity herself. With that philosophy, "The mail must go through," she gathered her children together, and largely with her own efforts and the inspiration from heaven she organized her oxen and equipment and drove a thousand miles over the prairies to the Salt Lake valley.

Just a little incident in that hazardous journey: Emigrant fashion, they were camped for the night. For fear her oxen would stray with other cattle owned by strangers who were driving for market, she left her oxen yoked for this particular night. In the morning her best yoke were missing. The men, along with her brother-in-law and son, all day had scoured every nook and corner of the river bank and the prairie for miles. Night was coming fast, and the hunters for the oxen, wet and exhausted, came into camp with no trace of the missing oxen. One hundred pounds of steer in their predicament was a mighty sacred parcel in the middle of the desert. It meant whether or not they would make it to the promised land.

Her son in approaching camp found his mother on her knees pouring out her soul to God for help. As she arose she met the discouragement of her son's face with a smile of confidence. She beckoned the all-day searchers to eat their supper. She was told by a herder that her cows had been seen a few hours before in a definite location. With a shawl over her shoulders she went in the opposite direction from the stranger's direction. In ten minutes she found the precious oxen in a clump of willows, and a few minutes later they went on their way with songs of thanksgiving on their lips, forging forward to the valley.

Bishop, such characters won the west. These humble but resolute characters have made history. They have made "Mormonism." Bishop, do you search for these sometimes unnoticed nuggets of gold?

Don't forget the silent mothers of the Joseph F. Smiths, the Widtsoes, and the Smoots. Let us ever remember that "the hand that rocks the cradle rules the earth." These silent unpretentious mothers sculptured character from the clay given them, and made history.

One half mile south of Sugar House in Salt Lake City, my friend Hyrum Jensen has placed a roof canopy over a humble adobe home that is a monument to one of the most sterling characters in the history of Mormonism. It is the original home of Mary Smith, the wife of Hyrum Smith, the martyred patriarch, the father of Joseph F. Smith. May that extra roof combat the elements that ordinarily would make short work of this dirt home! As the years roll on, may this humble abode remind all of us of the virtues, the firmness, devotion and, if you please, the fighting qualities of this indomitable woman.

We are still talking about these silent forces that make up the pillars of strength of any great cause in the world.

Dear reader, take time off long enough to read of the struggles of this Smith woman, especially the part she played in Church history after the death of her dear husband. If ever the Lord planted faith in one of his children, it was in this maker of history. With a self-reliance coupled with this child-like faith, she faced an avalanche of trouble thrown in her way.

Bishop, don't forget to put the proper value on the unpretentious—the meek and lovely—those who do not have themselves heralded with trumpets as they make their approach.

Bishop, there are people in your ward, unless you are very thoughful, who would jump for joy if you gave them a little more recognition.

No power or influence can or ought to be maintained by virtue of the priesthood, only by persuasion, by long suffering, by gentleness and meekness, and by love unfeigned. (D. & C., Sec. 121, Verse 41.)

This advice and a flock of such counsel has been burned into us for over a hundred years, but every once in a while you find a man with his authority going to his head. Yes, you'll find a fellow snapping his fingers at his "subjects," wanting to be obeyed like a despot on the throne. These fellows are few and far between and for this, their scarcity, we rejoice. But when we find a touch of this tendency to rule, we are reminded of its fallacy.

Bishop, do you get some apparent results because your

people fear you, or do you accomplish some *real* things because your people love you? Are you a driver with a lash or do your people respond to your love for them and the atmosphere you create by being thoughtful of them? You will accomplish ten times as much by encouraging them as by trying to drive them.

Bishop, are your people at ease when they are in your company or are they relieved when you have left? Remember, we are all human. People do their best work when they are at ease—not when they are rigid at attention. Don't regiment. You will be loved more if you get results by encouragement. We all do our best work when the boss taps us on the back with a "thank you."

I have a church leader in mind who as far as records are concerned is right up there. But those results are there because of pressure. I'm afraid he is more ambitious than he is devoted. When you make contact with his organization, you feel a tension, not a spirit of brotherly love and worship. Records are great things, but they are of no earthly good except as a means to an end. Don't work for records—but for results, and remember, your test as a bishop will be found in the extent with which your people love one another and you yourself.

The days of despotism are gone. The days of doing things by common consent are here to stay. We are speaking of nations; we are speaking of clubs, industries, and organizations of all kinds. We are speaking emphatically of this dear Church of ours. The man who thinks he can rule with an iron hand in this Church is doomed for an awfully short reign.

Great decisions are made only after proper ventilation of issues involved. Many minds make good decisions. As with a nation, this Church of ours, in a sense, is *of* the people, *by* the people, and *for* the people.

Bishop, no matter how firmly convinced you may be in the virtue of a stand you are taking, never force that conviction down the throats of your people. Let the people be heard, and you won't make any mistakes. Hear all sides of a question, honor those who may differ with you, take plenty of time to consider, and then with your counselors, after you have said your prayers, in a kindly way ask the people to support you.

Please examine the drawing accompanying this little chapter. Note the fellow on the throne with his adamant attitude. Now observe the other fellow at the head of the table with a smile on his face. Because of the atmosphere created by the latter, with a genial countenance he is calling for the best cooperation of those around him. The strength of the decisions made around that table will lie in the freedom of speech of those concerned and the pleasure each one gets in submitting his views on the subject.

The ad of a certain milk company has always impressed me. It was written right on their cans of prepared milk. The scene was a herd of beautiful cows grazing peacefully in a mountain dell. In big letters across the sky and over the beautiful landscape were these words:- "Contented cows give good milk." You know, these dairy people have made a careful study of milk production, and they know what they are talking about. I just know enough about this milk business and old Boss to know that if you whip and abuse her, you're going to get little milk, and the quality is going to be awfully poor.

Create a wholesome atmosphere, bishop, in your ward by a real democratic attitude and the results will be wonderful. On the other hand, whip, as it were, threaten, spank, and scold, and the pail of milk you get won't produce much butter.

Staying with this philosophy of contented cows giving good milk, you'll find the quality of the milk dependent very materially on the kind of food. Give those cows distasteful, bitter, wild clover, and you can't drink the milk and keep your face straight. (I've tried it, and I know what I'm talking about.) But lead the kine down into green, peaceful pastures and feed them on sweet clover, and you won't be able to supply the demand for your butter and milk.

Preside, bishop; but don't rule. Your people might take it a time or two, but it won't be long until there will be heard a rumbling that will reach to the high heavens. Yes, there'll be handwriting on the wall just as definitely as old Belshazzar saw the night in Babylon on his big twenty course feed when old Cyrus changed the course of the river under the gates of the city and marched in. "You have been weighed in the balance and have been found wanting, and the Medes and the Persians are knocking at your gates." Yes, bishop, as a leader your days will be numbered.

Bishop, if you rule instead of preside, every day of your administration will be marked with the hurt feeling of your people. No flower ever grown has more tender petals than are the souls of your people. The injury of a despotic thrust from you ofttimes cannot be healed in a lifetime. After all, you are dealing in this soul stuff.

It is just as impossible for you to retract your words and the harm they have done as it is to pick up the particles of egg, including the eggshell, mentioned in the Mother Goose rhyme of Humpty Dumpty.

Bishop, the most powerful implement you will use in your presidency will be kindness. It is more potent than the sharpest sword but never draws blood. It calls to mind but it doesn't wound. It teaches and corrects and the path it leaves is not one of hate and rebellion, but a flower-strewn lane of love and affection.

Bishop, if you rule, you'll be hated. Bishop, if you preside, you'll be loved.

STORY TWENTY-THREE

KINDNESS STRONGER THAN FORCE

This picture illustrates an old, old story. The sun and the wind one day got into an argument. In fact they were arguing as to which was the more powerful—the sun or the wind. If we may use our imagination, the conversation went about as follows:

The sun said, "There's a fellow going down the street. Let's see which of us can take his coat off first. Mr. Wind, you try first."

He did. He hit that fellow so hard with his gusts that the poor fellow pretty nearly was swept off the road, but the harder the wind blew the tighter did our friend pull his coat around him.

Force had failed.

"Now," said the sun, "let me try."

He did it the warm way. He threw his rays on that fellow's back, and in just a moment our friend's coat was off and being carried on his arm. Kindness had won.

Did you ever hear the story of the Bell Rock lighthouse? I heard it as I gazed on the lighthouse from the rocks of Scotland's shore. In Edinburgh's museum I saw the skeleton of the horse that dragged the stones that make up its walls. The Bell Rock is out about ten miles from shore. Even on a clear day, from the shore you see only, as it were, a tiny needle sticking out of the water. When the tide is out, the rock sticks its hideous head out of the water, fairly showing its teeth. But when the tide is in, its treachery is hidden. Many a seaworthy boat in time of storm was crashed from stem to stern and its contents of life and cargo fed to the ocean depths.

Some thoughtful monks determined to save life and property. They built a cradle-shaped boat and attached thereto a bell and chained the boat to the rocks. The more angry the waves, the greater the cry of the bell. It rang out for miles across the water—"Beware! Beware! Beware!" Many a life was saved. But pirates who profited from shipwrecked seamen determined they would put a stop to this warning. The more wrecks the greater booty for them! They pulled up the cradle boat and the chain that held it. Lives were again lost, and the pirates profited.

But this story has two chapters. Here's the second: These same robbers, at this very spot a few months later were caught in a terrific gale. Now, if only the cradle boat would ring! But it didn't. The tide was in, and the rock ambushed. They struck it, and all were lost! Now, as the light flashes from the top of that historic lighthouse, it seems to say, "Here is the evidence, cold and gray, To be unkind it just doesn't pay."

I believe it was Aesop who told the following story:

Mr. Frog met Mr. Mouse one day. Said the frog to his new friend, "Let's take a walk." The mouse accepted, and the two met the next day at an agreed spot on the field. The mouse had full confidence in his new friend and acquiesced to any suggestions, but the frog was bent on pulling a fast one on his unsuspecting friend. Now let's see what he was up to.

Said the frog, "Let's get a piece of string about a foot and a half long; then let's tie one end to your foot and one end to my foot." The mouse still having confidence in his host readily complied. They found the string and the operation was performed as per specifications suggested above. That's chapter one.

Chapter two: With the string between them they now continued their May day walk. Very soon they approached a shallow pond. The frog is now ready to pull his stunt. He springs the trap—in one big jump he lands in the pool. The mouse is only one tenth of the frog's weight, and, of course, glider fashion he sails through the air propelled by his "courteous" friend. They were still tied together. The mouse soon departed this life and floated on the top of the water—the frog gloating over his great stunt. (You know the frog is amphibious and can breathe under water as well as out in the open.)

That's the end of chapter two.

Chapter three: The game is not over yet. A hawk comes swooping over the swamp for his breakfast. His eagle eyes catch sight of the floating mouse. He made a speedy landing and came up with the mouse in his talons, but there was a string tied to the frog. The hawk had a rodent for his breakfast and an amphibian for his dinner.

Hitler played well the roll of the frog. Mussolini took well his part, too. The Japs, too, had a string tied to their legs when they swooped down on Pearl Harbor.

He who tries to injure others injures himself with his own setup.

The best weapon you carry is kindness. The strongest force in the world is the kind things you do to others.

My mother told me a story once I never forgot. It was about a fellow who had sticky fingers. (I'll try to make myself clear.) He went to a shop, and, when he thought the merchant was not looking, he lifted a pound of butter. He concealed it under a big stiff hat that he wore. It was in the days of beaver hats. Some merchants are like some schoolteachers—they have eyes in the back of their heads—the storekeeper knew where the pound of butter was.

Now, he's going to call the police—he's got him hands down. That's what you think. But the grocery man had another way of teaching that fellow a good lesson. Yes, he was going to turn on the heat but with kindness. It was winter. He led his friend over to the fire and with all the warmth of hospitality beckoned him to the stove. "Sit close up to the fire, John; it's a cold day." Yes, he put on the coal. The stove was a crimson red—so was John. Now John began to sweat. It wasn't a question of rendering lard, it was rendering kindness.

Well, now, the shop man got his butter back. The story is farfetched, I agree, but John will never again "worlds without end" make a larder of his hat.

STORY TWENTY-FOUR

MR. CHURCH OFFICER, DO YOU TALK TOO MUCH?

Mr. Church Officer, do you talk too much? You know, those over whom you preside have too much respect to tell you about it if you talk too much. There is nothing that will kill your prestige more than for you to be lecturing eternally to them. If you express yourself very easily and if you have real ability as a public speaker, you should ever be on your guard lest you comment too much from the pulpit. Many times you will be prompted to give vent to your feelings in lecturing, but be wise. Don't eternally "*spank*" your members. They will love you if you are frank; and you will never lose your influence, if, when an issue arises, you let them know where you stand, and further, point their noses in the right direction. You are wise—that's why you were chosen for leadership. To give advice from the pulpit or otherwise is your prerogative and your duty, but your people will take your advice more willingly if you don't *talk too much.*

One of the saddest things to find as one visits a ward is a "talking bishop." No matter what is said or done, he just must comment. Probably there is no place in a ward function where this is more noticeable than at a funeral. When an appropriate service has been rendered and everyone feels that the spirit is complete, it is often spoiled by an oration at the end. The spirit of many a wholesome service has been spoiled through a bishop's ambition to put the finishing touches on the program. Measure your words and let them be few. Don't have it said of you that the members of your organization are always using their faith and prayers to the end that you won't talk too much. Because your audience has its eye on you and has the attitude of being entertained, don't always suppose your message is sinking in. It won't sink in if you talk too much. Your listeners have too much respect for you to be discourteous. Their eyes may be riveted on you, but back of those eyes may be a prayer to heaven to bless you with more discretion than you are displaying in the moment of their boredom.

A story is told of a Negro preacher who was being visited at his church by a fellow pastor. Out of courtesy, the visitor was given a few moments to express himself from the stand. But I suppose the fellow pastor decided to take advantage of the invitation and talked an hour and a half. (He was like many people when called upon and thought he would make good use of the opportunity, as it might be a long while before the opportunity would knock at his door again.) Well, when he finished, there was only one thing to do, and that was to close the meeting. The prayer of the Negro preacher was about as follows: "Oh, Lord, we thank thee for our blessings and for the visit of our dear brother who has discoursed to us this day. Bless him, oh, Lord, and especially that he might take a few feathers from the wings of his imagination and place them on the tail of his judgment."

Remember the greatest constructive forces in the universe are silent. The boisterous noises like thunder are those that do the damage. The sun comes up each morning to give the earth its eternal vitality—silently. The worlds in the heavens do their work silently.

Your greatest generalship will be shown in distributing authority. Your leadership is measured by the type and caliber of men and women you draw about you. It is not measured by the noise you yourself make.

A visitor to a school was impressed with the discipline and the precision of the response of the pupils to their teacher. It was marvelous. Without any outward commotion, the students arose in unison and marched out as soldiers. In fact, the entire program was so orderly, and each one fitted his place in the program so well that the visitor was astounded. How did that teacher do it? The visitor was going to find out. After dismissal he accosted one of the boys of this unusual group of children where he had been visiting. Asked he, "How did all you boys and girls know when to arise? How did you all know so well when to march?" Then came the answer, "Didn't you see the teacher's thumb signal us?"

STORY TWENTY-FIVE

YOU CAN'T TAKE IT WITH YOU

This seems a ridiculous drawing, doesn't it? But the way you see some men plunging and driving for this stuff reminds us how peculiar must be the cerebral mechanics of their mental organizer of wealth, to a fellow like Henry Ford who by his wise manipulation of finance blesses the world. He blesses the man for whom he has furnished employment, and he blesses the man who buys his product. I am talking about the fellow who in a miserly way hoards his gold for the sake of accumulation alone. Some of these fellows get the mania so bad that their minds get really drunk, and they shut out the very sweetness of life itself.

Just imagine how hard it must be for this unfortunate fellow in the picture on the preceding page to die. "For where your treasure is, there will your heart be also."

When it comes down to good, hard terra firma sense, you've always got to go to the good Book. "Lay not up for yourselves treasures upon the earth, where moth and rust doth corrupt, and where thieves break through and steal."

Now from the looks of things the "poor" fellow in the illustration stacked all his treasures in the port that he is leaving There's another shore to which he's about to land where his inventory is not going to be too high. That's why he says he won't leave unless he can take his gold with him. But when the Great Reaper puts his hand on his shoulder and says, "come," he's going to go. And when he goes, he is going to leave everything. He can't even take with him an overnight bag.

If all of us would be more intent on accumulation of inventories over the horizon to meet us when we land over there, how much better world this would be. How much easier it would be for all of us to make the transition if we spent more time being kind and helping others than selfishly elbowing ourselves through life bent only on accumulation.

In a little eating place in New Mexico I couldn't help reading a little "handwriting on the wall" in this humble place. It read, "What a grand place this world would be, if I loved others like I love me."

You'd naturally think that men getting to that age when they'd be expecting a knock on their doors from the Great Sheriff of our destinies would want to direct their wealth into channels of doing good while they could get the thrill out of it. But too many just delight in seeing their pile get higher and higher, even when they close their eyes in the final earthly sleep. It's a strange psychology that is in the mind of a man about ready to make his final take-off. How many, many worthy causes would jump for joy if they were stimulated with financial encouragement from such a source as the one we are speaking about. It would seem to me on the part of the person able to do this kindness and yet not affect in any way his welfare in his closing days, that lending this aid would be a feeling that would "taste good all the way down."

I attended a banquet the other night where they picked up about $1,500.00 in their drive for funds for their contemplated new chapel. After the program was over the bishop came to me and said, "You know, Brother Ashton, with whom do you think we have the greatest trouble in a drive like this—that is, in separating people from their gold? It is with the man over seventy—the man who could never ordinarily spend his accumulation of wealth. It's easier," says he, "to get it from the younger man who has to budget himself very carefully."

You know, folks, this is quite an indictment. How much better it would be in many cases if just a little less were left to the children and more to a worth-while cause. Yes, there would probably be less fighting among offspring and more initiative put into their blood by giving them more reason to "grub, hog, or die."

This mania that men get sometimes could very easily be labeled a disease. Like an octopus it gets the half nelson on its victim, and the latter is going to the mat for the "ten count" if he isn't very careful. Again it's a matter of habit. "Habit is a cable. We weave a thread of it each day, and soon it becomes so strong we cannot break it." Yes, it works nearly as automatically as reflex action. It gets right into our blood and controls us.

Yes, it's a habit of grabbing, grabbing, grabbing. Let me illustrate:- A fellow of this grabbing make-up was working on a ripsaw. In pushing a two by four through his machine one day off came a finger. Instead of letting his fellow workman rush him to first aid this peculiar fellow persisted in fingering around in the sawdust for his lost finger. While so employing himself. "Zip," there goes another one. Now he had two fingers somewhere in that sawdust, more persistent than ever now in excavating sawdust for the lost members of his anatomy. His friends could no more pull him away than they could fly. The other workmen in standing around were afraid he would bleed to death, but yet the grabbing propensities of our victim urged him on stronger than ever, searching that sawdust for the fingers.

But an acquaintance of our bleeding friend came to the rescue. He knew him well. He knew of his life of grabbing. He inquired what was the excitement. They told him. Yes, he knew our ripsaw friend like a book. "Oh," said he, "if that's all you're worried about, I can fix that."

He put his hand in his pocket, pulled out a quarter, threw it into the bloodsoaked sawdust. Immediately the two lost fingers came out of their hiding and grabbed the silver like a trout taking a fly.

I repeat, that was reflex action.

One of the saddest pictures we have in the Church (and we who go to a different stake about every week know what we are talking about) is the man holding an important position in the Church who has this disease about which we are talking. You find a fellow racing through life, every nerve bent in the direction of accumulation of wealth, and his Church work just gets the crumbs of his energy. Yes, and his organization seems to go ahead in spite of his neglect of the more important things of life. But if that same fellow would give the

Lord just a fair portion of his capacity, the Church in his direction would go in leaps and bounds.

"Lay up yourselves treasures in heaven, where neither moth nor rust doth corrupt."

STORY TWENTY-SIX

DON'T BE HASTY

Some of the stories our mothers have told us stay with us through life, don't they? The accompanying illustration tells a story my mother told me as a youngster. Don't be hasty. Weigh things carefully before you strike. When your blood pressure gets up, count ten. "School Thy Feelings, Oh, My Brother" is one of the best bits of advice ever given. Beware of mistakes made in taking too seriously circumstantial evidence. Think before you act. Don't forget that truth is very often stranger than fiction.

May I remind you in just a few words the facts of the story above.

This trapper's wife was brought to the Alaska wilderness. She was cut down by death. Their child was about two years old. To go out in the woods in the course of his trapping, the trapper had sometimes left the child for a few hours in the care of their faithful dog. On such an absence one afternoon a terrible blizzard came up. The storm was so terrible that he had to take refuge in a hollow tree to save his life. At daybreak he rushed to his cabin. The door was open. His dog who looked at him from the corner of his eyes was covered with blood. The father's blood froze in his veins. Just one thing had happened—his dog had turned wolf and had killed his child. He reached for the ax, and in a moment the same was buried into the skull of his trusted animal.

Like a maniac he scanned the scene. In hopeless desperation he uncovered the gruesome remnants of his cabin. Tipped over, the cracked furniture was telling a story of a battle that had taken place here an hour before. A faint cry came from under the bed. Again his heart seemed paralyzed. There he found his offspring safe and sound. Just a moment of pause to cuddle his dear one in his arms and he was off to determine whence the blood on his dog came. The answer came just a second later. The sad riddle was solved. In a remote corner, there it was—a dead wolf, his huge mouth showing fangs intended for the baby which his faithful dog had saved.

Just a moment of caution and he could have held both his babe and his hero dog in his arms. Remorse took over instead.

In one of the old readers we used to read a story really a twin sister to the above:

In the old days of hunting, before gunpowder was invented, when bows and arrows were used, in some spots of Europe falcons were trained to help them in the hunt. This bird is a species of hawk, and, if we are to believe history, these fellows were really faithful and efficient. The falcon would soar into the air, survey the country round about, and, if he discovered the deer, with the shriek of his voice or the flap of his wings, he guided his master to the game.

Now the king had been out hunting with his fellow noblemen but he had got lost. In fact he had separated from his friends and the commissary department two days before. He had with him his trained falcon that rested on his wrist. The king was nearly starved to death as was the bird but worse than the call for food was his thirst. He got so desperate for water that he would have eaten mud. His tongue was as thick as leather; his eyes were bulging with concern; his eyes had desperately scanned every rock for some signs of moisture. He and his falcon were pretty nearly dead. The monarch could hardly pull one foot in front of the other.

But lo and behold, off a hundred yards he detected something that looked like dripping water! It was! New strength came into his veins. He automatically leaped forward with the cup he always carried with him, the falcon, of course, ever present on his wrist.

Drip, drip, drip, and the cup was finally full. The king was just putting it to his lips when his falcon knocked the cup from his hands. Had the bird gone crazy? He'd fill it again—he did. With one eye on the hawk and one on the cup, for the second time he raised it to his lips, but for the second time it was knocked from his grasp.

The king unsheathed his sword. He talked to his friend that had been so faithful to him up to now. "You do that again, and off comes your head."

Drip, drip, drip for the third time. Did you ever hold a pigeon in your hands? Their strength is really astonishing. When you talk about their wing strength, and especially if he uses his claws, a hawk is a piece of dynamite. For the third time the falcon was on the job watching his master and that newly filled cup. As the hunter raised the water to his lips, in some super way the bird got loose, clawed the hands of the king, and knocked the life-saving, sparkling water to the desert floor.

The king had made a promise, and the ruler's word must be kept. He had promised the bird he would take his life if he pulled the stunt once more. Out came the sword—off came the head of the falcon. As the parched earth absorbed in itself the blood of his before now precious hawk, the king scratched his forehead; he was thinking. What in the world had possessed his feathered servant? He would make an investigation.

Once again his eyes followed those precious drops of water as they trickled down the rock. "I'll climb up there." It only took a minute, and he was at the source of the miniature spring. He turned ghastly pale. He nearly fainted at what he saw in that hollow rock whence came that drip, drip, drip.

Taking up a great part of the stagnant pool was coiled a poisonous snake that had been dead for weeks. The water while it sparkled over the rocks was cankered with the virus of the serpent. That handful of water meant "dead men's bones."

Hesitantly the king retraced his steps and now gazed on the lifeless form of his feathered hero, but too late. His temper had ruled him. "All the king's horses and all the king's men" couldn't put that falcon's head back again and start again the flow of blood that soaked the sand to course again through its sacred body. The bird had been flying over those hills for two days. His viewpoint was better than the king's whose experience had been confined to the domain covered by his feet only.

"Think before you leap," or as Davy Crockett put it, "Be sure you're right and then go ahead." Don't be hasty.

Speaking of circumstantial evidence, I am reminded of an experience we had in Scotland as missionaries. A very splendid lady, her husband, and whole household, left the Church because she, like the king we have been talking about and the hunter who slew his faithful dog, took snap judgment and pulled the trigger. My heart aches when I think of the ruinous results that followed her hastiness. Her name was Jack, and she lived in Dundee. We missionaries had been there six months and had baptized the whole family at conference time for the Scotch mission. We left Dundee to attend the conference in Glasgow. This Sister Jack wanted to come to the conference, too, and another missionary and I agreed to meet her at the railroad station.

We were in a meeting when we were to leave for the depot, keeping track by our watches so we would be there on time. While in that meeting someone put his head in the door and whispered, "Sister Jack has arrived." Well, we who were to be at that railroad station sat back and relaxed with this thought: "Sister Jack has taken an earlier train, and we can stay longer in our meeting."

But what were the facts of the case we found when our meeting dismissed? Another Sister Jack from another part of Scotland had arrived at the conference house, and while we were contenting ourselves that all was well, the other Sister Jack from Dundee had arrived and was pacing up and down the railroad platform muttering unkind things about a pair of Mormon missionaries that had double-crossed her.

Well, that good lady took the next train back to Dundee, told the story to her family, and left the Church. To this day, if that Scotch lady is still on mother earth, she thinks that we double-crossed her with malice aforethought.

Circumstantial evidence sometimes is the cruelest thing that exists.

Don't be hasty.

May I hurriedly recall to you a sad story told by Longfellow in "Evangeline":

Many years ago in an old city of Europe whose name is not given, the people raised a brass statue of Justice in the public square. Upholding this statue were outstanding columns. In the left hand of the statue was held the scales of Justice, and in the right hand a sword as an emblem that Justice would be enforced all over the land. Even the birds built their nests in the scales of the balance.

As the story goes, in the course of time the laws of the land were corrupted. At this later time a necklace in the home of a nobleman was lost. An orphan girl who worked at this home was accused of the deed and condemned to die on the scaffold. There she actually met her doom—right at the foot of the statue of Justice. Years afterwards a great tempest arose in the city and lightning smote the bronze statue. The huge structure fell to the pavement breaking it into a thousand pieces. In the scales of the balance which were shattered to the pavement were found the remnants of an old magpie's nest, and in this nest lay the necklace of pearls stolen many years before.

Somebody had taken snap judgment. Somebody had taken too seriously circumstantial evidence.

STORY TWENTY-SEVEN

IS THERE A GULF BETWEEN US AND OUR CHILDREN?

The other day in calling at a farmhouse, I observed in the big yard a picture about like the accompanying sketch.

I don't believe the fellow who put those duck eggs under that unsuspecting hen realized what nervous tension the mother would be under a few weeks later. As soon as the old hen left the nest with her brood, lo and behold, they made for the water! In a jiffy they acted as if they had had six months' training in swimming, diving, and aquatic gymnastics. Please note the good time they are having splashing about, and then look at the consternation of that poor parent. In plain American English, she's a nervous wreck, and they're in ecstasy. They are in a merry world, following the impulses of youth—she is in a world of fretting and stewing. In other words, there is a gulf between her and her children.

Now don't take all the details of this comparison too literally or this illustration will miss the mark. But, when I see parents who do not understand the frolics of youth and want to hold the youth to the confines of the tendencies of adults, I think of that old hen with her ducklings. Those little fellows with their heads under water won't drown; they'll come up. That little urchin scampering to the outer edge of the pool will get back. One of the saddest things in life is to find parents who either never had a normal childhood or forget what they liked to do as children. It is a good thing for some parents that they do forget what they used to do or they'd wake up sometime with a nightmare.

A father, unconscious of his own status, was heard to say, "My son will be the worst rascal in town when I die." His friend, whose memory was a little better, exclaimed, "Yes, but not until then." Mr. and Mrs. Parent, do you have the viewpoint of youth, or are you lacking the sympathy for youth that makes you loved by them? If you have faith in youth, half of your troubles are over.

Probably no man who has graced our Church history loved youth more than William A. Morton. He had great influence with them because he understood them. He told a beautiful story of an old cat and her kittens. He was stopping at a lodging house in Liverpool. While sitting in the dining room one day, his attention was called to this mouser and her half-grown family on the floor near him. Mrs. Cat was having quite a time with a gray and white member of her active brood which was always getting into mischief. It tangled up the yarn, climbed up the tablecloth, and nearly knocked a plate and saucer off the shelf. Brother Morton said it was amusing to see the old mother cat continually go up to the unruly member of her family and correct it by slapping it on the head with her paw. The prodigal kitten was so interesting in her capers that, he says, the distinctiveness of the kitten from its brothers and sisters was vividly impressed upon him. He could not forget its gray and white markings.

The interesting part of this story is that Brother Morton called at the same lodging a year later. Again he was entertained by a cat and her brood on the dining room floor. What held his attention even more was that this time the mother cat who took the center of the stage was gray and white—yes, the kitten who a year ago had been making life so unpleasant for its serious mother, was now the mother. History was repeating itself—the grown-up gray and white cat was now up in arms in her responsibilities with a black member of her brood which was trying to tear down the house. The new mother was slapping her unruly black kitten on the head, trying to keep it in the line of good behavior.

How like the life of us human beings is this story of the cats. Let's not lose faith in that youngster. Let's hold on to him. Let's be tolerant and patient. Ever keep in mind that there was as much human nature with young folk in our generation as there is with the new generation which is worrying us now.

I hope I shall never forget the impressions along this line made upon me as a boy by our old neighbor in the Fifteenth Ward. His name was Ben Guiver. Blessed be his name! How many who read this page remember the days of the old ugly valentine? Do you men in your fifties remember how you used to treat the front doors of your neighbors' houses with your feet on Valentine's night? Of course, we didn't do those good-looking doors any good by the time we had finished with them. Yes, we were thoughtless—most kids are. If we had used our knees on those doors when we left the valentine there, it wouldn't have made enough noise. We applied our thick-soled shoe tips to the doors. Yes, I blush about it now, but it is too late to feel bad; we were kids and didn't think. The neighbors got up in arms, and then there was open season on some of us—almost a bounty on our scalps.

But what did our neighbor Guiver do? Did he stand around the corner of his house February 14 from 6 p.m. to 12 midnight with a six-shooter? Oh, no! He understood human nature and understood "*kid nature*." A couple of days before the night when war was to be declared on front doors, he went to an old shed in the rear of his house and brought out an old dilapidated door and put it upright in front of his varnished door. There were no hieroglyphics written on the door but in great big letters visibly written were the words: "There it is boys; kick the daylights out of it." And we did. Did we love Benjamin Guiver? We did.

Don't rub your boy the wrong way. Study him and be patient with him and make some allowances.

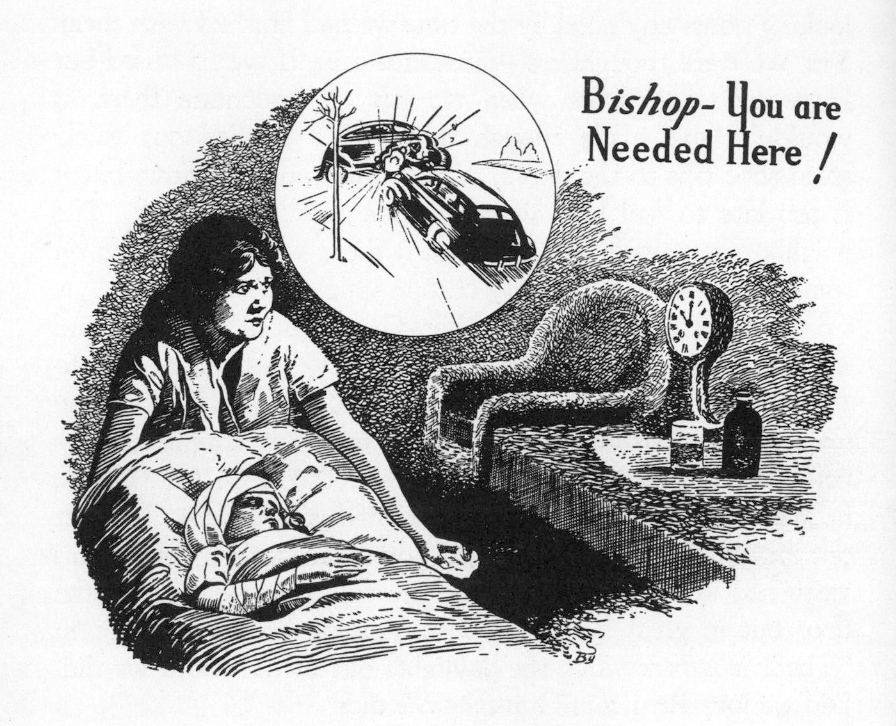

STORY TWENTY-EIGHT

Bishop, there's trouble here—they need you! When there are tugs at the heart, that's when they need the father of the ward. There's been an accident here, and this little child hovers between life and death. If there is any spot where you are appreciated tonight, it is in this home. Ward budgets are important; keeping the quorums on schedule will have to be stressed; and many other responsibilities that are yours can't be neglected; but of all the things under your domain, nothing is more important than your taking sunshine and comfort to those who mourn. Bishop, the clasp of your hand in such a home does wonders, in fact, no other by virtue of your particular calling has such a healing balm.

The Church will look to you for progress in keeping up with the times, the Lord will expect you to be on your toes in doing things that show you are not in a rut, but of all the things the heavens will be slow to forgive you for will be in your neglect in making those calls to those in distress. No responsibility you have should take precedence over them. Delegate all the authority you can. The more you do along this line the more efficient will be your administration, but never pass to the other fellow the responsibility of that kindly touch that is only yours, as we say again, as father of your flock. In trouble no hand clasp or pat on the shoulder is quite as effective as yours. Bishop, you may get praise for efficiency in this or that, and your name may be tacked up high in the attainments of your ward, but nothing will call for your people to call your name blessed more than that you are considered to be human in your greatest responsibilities.

I am reminded of the life of a man whose birthday we celebrate. We don't make it a holiday today because he split rails. We have something more weighty to think about than just ceasing from our ordinary labors because we want to remember a man who pulled a pig out of the mud, but the greatness of that man was in his sympathy for his fellows, coupled with his being one of the greatest thinkers of his time or any other time. He dared to do the common things. Whenever you found him at the crossroads where he was to choose between the kind thing or the thing that might in a sense be more apparently conspicuous, he always made a bee-line with no hesitancy to that spot pleading for a human touch.

Bishop, let me illustrate: Lincoln was running for Congress. His prospects were good. His political antagonist, as politicians will do, ripped him up the back and belittled him in the eyes of his countrymen. A big meeting was scheduled a few nights ahead when people would come by the thousands to hear the rail splitter defend himself. I suppose of all meetings a man would want to attend, it would be the occasion when he could clear himself, and Lincoln was a past master in convincing people of his being, as he put it, "on God's side." But about two days before this important rally a little thing happened to change the mind of this big fellow about whom we are speaking. A little woman that day left a note on the desk of this home-spun country lawyer. When he came back to his office and discovered the letter, his place on that all-important program ahead was canceled. The only answer his campaign manager could get was, "I won't be making that talk tomorrow night." And the future emancipator said it with a fixed eye and set jaw that meant to his political boss that he might just as well try to change the course of the Mississippi as to try to change his mind.

And the six foot-four-inch woodsman didn't change his mind. There was another place calling a little louder than political rallies. The call came from the humble cottage of the little woman who dropped that note on his desk. There was trouble by that fireplace. Yes, there was a debt to that abode he was to pay in the next couple of days. Congress, fame, and all their trimmings were like pigmies compared to the attraction out in the country twenty miles away. Sink or swim, survive or perish, the rawboned lawyer would be there.

Next morning as the sun stuck his head over the horizon he looked down on a lanky form climbing fences and with a determined stride covering the distance between himself and a little courthouse far into the woods.

Let's not go into detail—the story is gripping. You'll find it in a little book *Counsel Assigned.*

When he arrived at 10:00 o'clock, the courtroom was jammed. Those backwoods folk were good people, but they wanted to see the law take its course even if a sixteen-year-old lad was up for murder, and the penalty might be death.

The big man who cut through the fields that morning so early and ate his breakfast from his pocket, defended the boy. The boy was working for a hard taskmaster farmer. In a cruel moment he had pricked the boy's legs with the business end of a pitchfork. In the heat of retaliation the boy took the fork from his antagonist, and in the tussle a prong entered the brain of the unwise farmer. But, I repeat, those people wanted justice no matter what.

As that big frame faced that farmer jury, that sad but kindly face broke forth with something like this: "Gentlemen, when God calls, sometimes in answering his call we have to make sacrifices. Gentlemen, today I have made the sacrifice. Gentlemen, the father and mother of this youth on trial today were a father and mother to me when others shut their doors on the plea of a young man trying to make his own living in the world. I told God if he'd give me a chance I'd pay the bill. Gentlemen, this is the first day I've had a chance to pay that bill."

Well, when the verdict of "innocent" rang through that stuffy room of justice, one of those big arms got the mother, and the youth proclaimed innocent swooned into the warmth of the other.

Lincoln lost the election. He didn't go to Washington. He made the sacrifice—he paid the price, he was just another step further into the heart of the American people who put a premium on the man that dares to do the common things.

Yes, you can fool "some of the people all of the time,

and all of the people some of the time, but you can't fool all of the people all of the time." Truth crushed to earth shall rise again.

Bishop, dare to do the old-fashioned, common things. I repeat, you are most needed where "there are tugs at the heart." If there is trouble in that home, cross its threshold with the comfort that only you as an ordained bishop to his people can give.

STORY TWENTY-NINE

MR. LEADER OF BOYS, ARE YOU TALKING TO THEM OR OVER THEM?

Are you stressing attendance and records and forgetting to "feed" those sheep—our boys? Are you talking their language? Are they on the edge of their seats to get every morsel of what you are giving them, or are they yawning and turning to look at the clock? Are they praying that you'll soon quit talking or do they pray that the clock will move slowly? Is your approach "up the alley" or is what you are thundering at them as dry as the Sahara? You know, brethren, those little fellows are so loyal and respectful to you they won't tell you they are bored. Let's be dead sure when those fine thoroughbred "colts" come into the "stall," there is appetizing hay in the manger. If there is, they'll be eager to come back; if there is not, you'll have to get a "block and tackle" to pull them in.

Does this picture remind you of your leadership? Are these your boys? Is this you? Are you loaded with information and stories that appeal to those splendid young fellows? Are you inspiring them with those things you liked when a boy or is your appeal dry and parched? Is what you are giving them right "fresh out of the oven" or is it warmed-over from the other meals? Is the water fresh from the well or is it from a stagnant pool that gags the little fellows? We are sure that we are responsible to a great extent for that great multitude of vigorous fellows over twenty-one still holding only the Aaronic Priesthood. As Roscoe Gilmore Stott has put it, "In fishing for these boys, are we using the right bait?"

I repeat it, are we dry?

Once in a while you will find someone brave enough to tell you what he thinks. I had that experience about a year ago while attending a stake conference. Blessed be that good brother who opened up to me the inner workings of his mind. It was the welfare meeting—the last of the conference. Most of the time in this meeting was given to reports from the Relief Society on the latest developments in the dehydration of food. These ladies had just attended a government convention where they had heard the latest chapter on dehydration. They showed us at this meeting that with one tenth of the tin now used in canning peaches, we could preserve the same amount of fruit by drying it. They made it clear to us that with one tenth of the price now paid for freight, we could transport the same amount of dried produce. Well, to say the least, that was a revelation to me. These good folks had been in meeting for two days, and they had had about enough preaching. I thought I had some inspiration and shot out at them something like this: "Now, brothers and sisters, don't you think one of the finest projects the Church could get into would be the dehydration of speeches?" I thought I'd thrown a ringer, but I had put my chin out a little too far. Did you ever have that experience? A good brother sitting on the second row quietly and respectfully resounded, "Brother Ashton, don't you think the speeches are about dry enough as they are?"

Well, I still contend our speeches should be dehydrated, but I believe our brother was right—*they're dry enough.* Especially with fine boys, our talks should be more carefully studied, and invigorating. They've got to be more spicy. Yes, they need more vitamins and ginger. If that boy is inattentive, blame yourself, not him.

The following story is scripture to me. I'll never forget it. Its philosophy sticks to me like glue. I picked it up in Scotland while on a mission there. Sandy would go to sleep in church. This didn't please the minister. The latter stood it for several Sundays, and then he decided he'd burn Sandy up about it. He did.

"Sandy, you must stay awake. It looks terrible to go to sleep—it sets a bad example."

Sandy replied, "I canna help it."

The minister said, "But you must help it."

Sandy answered, "But I canna help it."

The minister thought he had an inspiration and said: "Sandy, next Sunday bring a bit o' snuff. When you feel yourself getting drowsy, just put a pinch of it in your nose."

Now Sandy was inspired, "Mr. Minister, do you not think it would be an awful guid plan if you'd put a wee bit o' snuff into your sermons?"

STORY THIRTY

'Twas a sheep not a lamb
That strayed away in the parable Jesus told,
A grown-up sheep that strayed away from the ninety and nine in the fold.
And why for the sheep should we seek and as earnestly hope and pray?
Because there is danger when sheep go wrong:
They lead the lambs astray.
Lambs will follow the sheep, you know,
Wherever the sheep may stray.
When sheep go wrong,
It won't take long till the lambs are as wrong as they.
And so with the sheep
We earnestly plead
For the sake of the lambs today,
For when sheep are lost
What a terrible cost
The lambs will have to pay.

Author Unknown

How in the world do you expect much from a son who has a dad who is not setting the right example. "As father so son"—yes, and let's go on, "As mother so daughter." "They step in our footsteps all the way."

As has been observed time and time again by those who ought to know, it isn't a question of youth delinquency—it's the problem of the parents going "the straight and narrow."

Parents, you make yourself look silly when you sit down to give your boy or girl counsel and don't practice what you preach. If you folks get in at two o'clock in the morning, that's when they will be pulling in. If you are pulling on a cigarette and drinking your cocktails, your offspring will take the same chance as you folks at drunken driving.

Dad, you are or ought to be your son's ideal. Whatever you do is right to him. What earthly good is it for you to stand with him at the crossroads of life if you are doing the very things that lead to that "angry snare."

JUST LIKE HIS DAD

He wants to be like his Dad! You men,
Did you ever think, as you pause,
That the boy who watches your every move
Is building a set of laws?
He's molding a life you're the model for,
And whether it's good or bad,
Depends on the kind of example set
To the boy who'd be like his dad.
Would you have him go everywhere you go?
Have him do just the things you do?
And see everything that your eyes behold,
And woo all the gods you woo?
When you see the worship that shines in the eyes
Of your lovable little lad,
Could you rest content if he gets his wish
And grows to be like his dad?

Author Unknown

I repeat a story (what good is a story if you can't use

it twice?) The mother who couldn't get her little daughter to bed said, "Mary, don't you know that all those little chickens went to bed hours ago?" "Yes, ma, but the old hen went with them, didn't she?"

You must set the right example, and if you don't, your children won't listen to you. When you are talking, they will be thinking of something else—"How can I believe what you say when what you are thunders in my ears?"

A mother was once giving her girl the lecture of her life. I guess the daughter needed it, but because the mother herself didn't come clean, her talk didn't go over. Yes, the child looked steadfastly into her mother's face every moment of the lecture—her face, as it were, was glued to that of her enthusiastic mother. The mother thought every drop of her discourse had sunk into the depths of her child's understanding. But get the reaction when the curtain lecture was over. Instead of a reaction of repentance, here came the observation of the daughter: "Ma, when you talk, your upper jaw don't move at all, does it?"

When we talk, what we *are* thunders in the ears of our listeners.

In Scotland many ministers make no bones at all about drinking. Some of them take their "wee drap" as habitually as they do their meals. Well, this minister about whom I am talking this particular morning had taken his usual dram. Immediately thereafter he made his usual visit to the hospital to cheer up the sick. I suppose he was at a particular old man's bed just a few minutes after his indulging himself with John Barleycorn. (Am I making myself clear?) The old man listened, apparently very earnestly, as the minister leaned over and read from the scriptures. As the Scotch pastor got close to the old gentleman our sick friend raised up on his elbows in order to get to the parson's face. When he had finished the first reading, our hospital patient called for a second reading. The minister read it a second time, and, when he had finished, the old man strained himself to get closer to the face of his spiritual advisor.

But lo and behold, after the story had been read, not once but twice, to the utter surprise of our visiting brother the sick man asked that the story be told for the third time! By the time he had read it for the third time our old friend on the cot had got so close to the entertaining minister that their faces almost touched. Never before had our evangelist been so impressed with a message he'd tried to put over. He stopped, set his book down, and addressed his listener as follows: "I've read that story of the Prodigal Son three times. Now what I want to know is what part of the story interested you most."

Please study closely, dear reader, just what was interesting our patient—here is his answer: "Mister Minister, I used to work in the mines. Ye ken, I used to have a *wee drap* myself—*your breath is grand.*"

STORY THIRTY-ONE

Yes, he's now coming home. He's returning with a scar "brought from some well won field." Let us pray that our eyes will not be dim in their appreciation of what he has done for us. It was Chief Justice Hughes who said that each generation must pay the price of liberty. Maybe in the great philosophy of things it is not a mistake that we do have to pay continually for this priceless blessing "liberty."

We all couldn't go to the front, so we sent that boy we're talking about. Because he bared his breast to the enemy's bullets he may come home with scars. They may not be the result of a bullet nor a thrust of a bayonet. They may be scars from other battles, other than powder and steel. But just the same they will be scars.

I ask you, dear brother and sister in this Church, are you going to criticize him unmercifully for some apparent weaknesses or are you going to be big enough to sense what he has done for you and what gratitude you owe him? Hadn't we better, with all the charity and kindness in the world that Christ tried to teach us, with a "God bless you," put your arms around him? Don't forget this—you might have kept yourself lily-white as far as some of the commandments are concerned, but when the moment called for you and me to charge the ramparts and face the pillbox, we might have failed and yielded. Again I remind you, it's the sense of proper values.

Some people just must have scriptures to be convinced. To them I quote from Him who tried to get us to think straight. "*And why beholdest thou the mote that is in thy brother's eye, but considerest not the beam that is in thine own eye?*" Might we add what you see on some signs, "THIS MEANS YOU!"

When this fellow comes home, that's when he'll need the Church, and that's when he'll need his friends . . . yes, if you please, that's when we should put our arms around him. Let the fervor of our love for him over-shadow some of the habits he might have picked up while fighting for us. Remember Christ said that no man is greater than he who gives his life for his friend.

Let us be perfectly frank—"When Johnnie comes marching home"—what are you going to do about him? If ever he needed the Church, it is now. Remember, "Judge not the workings of his brain, And of his heart thou canst not see." Remember it is through the sacrifice that he has made that our homes and ideals are preserved and that we worship God according to the dictates of our conscience.

Great hearts have made history. You can't think of liberty without thinking of a character so bold and brave as to say to his men, "We beat them today or Molly Stark is a widow." Yes, when we think liberty, we see a brave patriot walking up and down the ramparts of Bunker Hill inspiring his men with "Don't shoot till you see the whites of their eyes." A glorious moment is in vision when we contemplate, "Don't give up the ship;" "Give me liberty or give me death." We experience goose flesh in the words heard around the world, "All I regret is that I have only one life to give for my country."

When you contemplate the victories of U. S. Grant, necessary to bring about a united nation, do you magnify his failings? Let us ever hold in the background the weaknesses of those brave fellows who faced hot lead on the bloody beach of Tarawa. Let's pinch ourselves to a realization of the debt of gratitude we owe their courage.

Just a little story:—It is a backwoods school. The teacher and the boy are not on the best of terms. The boy has done something that has raised the ire of the teacher. The situation is so tense that the teacher vehemently follows the boy to his home. Right or wrong, the lad is standing his ground. The teacher, upon entering the gate is met by the boy's pal, "Towser," the dog. The dog's instructions from his master have been so well obeyed that the teacher has to make for a tree. When he tries to come down, the dog takes the situation in hand so well that the teacher confines himself to the upper limbs of the tree. The boy's instructions are to the dog, "Watch him, Towser!"

"Ma" tries to call off the dog. "Pa" joins in. All the neighbors try to call off the animal, but it is a one man's dog, and as the faithful animal hears his instructions, "Watch him, Towser!"—the teacher stays in the tree.

The boy thinks he is right, and all the powers of persuasion of family and neighbors won't call off the dog. We didn't say the boy was right, but there was something unusual burning in the boy's bosom that told him that as long as he thought himself right, he was going to stay with his convictions no matter what pressure was brought to bear.

Furthermore, we didn't say the teacher was wrong. Nine times out of ten a teacher is right. All we are trying to bring out is the courage of the boy—right or wrong—to stand by his guns.

Now, will you please shift gears with me for just a moment? It is one of those big battles of the Civil War. It is in the Shenandoah Valley—that valley where General Early took such big tolls from the North. Over the distant hills twenty miles away comes the boom of the cannon. The Union General leaps on his famous steed—the race is on!

I saw the play. I saw the horse lathered from head to foot, nostrils extended, carry his gallant rider into the fray. The men have been retreating all day. With unsheathed sword pointed to heaven, the little fellow on that famous horse gives command to his discouraged men—"We are going back!" The men wheeled about—turned rout into victory. It was one of those battles that turned the tide of the war. A great victory was won that day.

You will find the bones of that wonderful steed preserved in a New York museum: Who was his rider? Who was it that turned defeat into victory? Who was that fellow loved by his fellows for his undaunted courage whose words, "Boys, we're going back" electrified them? It was Gen. Phil Sheridan—the boy in the backwoods school who had the audacity to stand off the whole neighborhood. Yes, with his teeth set, he had the audacity to instruct his dog-pal, "Watch him, Towser!"

Back to our text, "Judge not the workings of his brain." When you discount him for an apparent flaw in his make-up, don't you dare crumble to the earth that quality so much in demand these days and in every age—*courage*.

We are stressing again this sense of values. When that boy comes home, let us put our arms around him and let him feel there is a place in the Church and in our hearts for him. Yes, and let's emphasize this—that much more glory and credit goes to the boy that remembers the standards of his father and mother and the Church. Yes, he faced death, too—and *he* did not faint and yield. And he has battles back of him that we won't have to fight.

STORY THIRTY-TWO

The drawing illustrates a story I suppose all of us have heard since we were children, but as ridiculous as the story is there is some real philosophy here. It's just another way of saying "Hitch your wagon to a star" or our accomplishments are dependent on our ideals. Where we have no ideals, we crawl on the ground. While this poor little bantam hen is going to have quite a time in laying an egg the size of that laid by the ostrich, in life what we amount to depends in a great big way on the urge that eternally hangs in front of us.

What has been done can be done. There is no greater

stimulus in the world than traveling. We ought to know continually what our neighbors are doing. Speaking of chickens and the size of eggs they lay reminds me of a story President Stayner Richards used to tell.

Nothing will keep us out of a rut more than visiting our neighbors. That neighbor may be the fellow who lives next door to us or a civilization across the Atlantic or the Pacific. If we see what our neighbor is doing, it helps to keep us out of the swamps of life. When we see what he is doing, it is just human nature to set our sails in the same direction and try to accomplish the same as he.

Now this story about chickens: It seems that a school was located next to a farm, there being a fence to mark the Mason and Dixon line between the two activities. Near every farm, of course, there must be a flock of hens with the usual rooster absolute monarch of all his domain. Now at recess the boys of the school were playing football. (Please keep in mind the shape of that inflated pigskin and how well its oval shape contributes to its being carried under a boy's arm.) Well, in the kickoff the fellow doing this particular job just got too energetic. Instead of the ball alighting where it should within the confines of the school property, it sailed through the air and bounced in the vicinity of this rooster and his respectful harem. Just as soon as this proud fellow saw the football he stopped and noticing both its size and shape, he rushed to the big egg-shaped leather. In just a moment, according to his call, every hen in his kingdom was standing surrounding the ball curiously inspecting this familiar shaped but new article. When all his subjects were at attention, he observed to them in no unmistakable language, "Well, hens, you see what our neighbors are doing."

I repeat, if we all were made better acquainted with what our neighbors are doing we would be "laying a bigger egg," if you please. We would be more alert and more on our toes to our responsibilities.

This means you, Mr. governor of a state; you, Mr. mayor of a town; and you, Mr. principal of a school. Yes, it means you, superintendent of a mill or a bishop of a ward or a superintendent of a Sunday School. You who have the responsibility of the youth, see what your neighbors are doing.

We should do more visiting. To see what others are doing by visiting is better than reading a book of instructions. Eternally keep using your ground by planting wheat or your land will go back to sagebrush. Don't stop in your churning or the butter will go back, too. (I found that out as a boy when I used to churn for my mother.) When you see a thing well done in the line of your work, get a "half nelson" on that idea quickly and use it. Let us continually say our prayers and ask the heavens to help us, but remember always the Lord expects us to "paddle our own canoe." Keep things stirring—running water never gets stagnant. The story has been told so many times that it's pretty trite, but let's eat the story for breakfast once in a while. It will do us no harm.

The stranger interested in a well-kept farm remarked to its owner, "You and the Lord have done a real job on this desert spot."

"Yes," says the energetic farmer, "but you should have seen this place when God tried to do it himself."

No matter who we are or what the color of our eyes, we all need a continual shot in the arm. If we are not careful our batteries get down, and we get as sluggish and morbid as the Malad River. If we're not careful, we will get like a turtle—we're dead and don't know it. Every once in a while we need to have retreads on our intellectual tires. You'll never get rusty if like the bee you go from flower to flower to get the sweetness and fragrance there found.

THIS IS NO TIME TO BE BLIND

This is an age of readjustment. Only those capable of making quick changes fit the times. Those with closed eyes and closed minds are in for trouble.

A blind man wants the furniture in a room left unchanged. Only then can he move about with any degree of comfort and safety. Change the setting, and he finds himself bumping into things. No longer can he move freely.

In our Church there are many men who act as if they were blind. They, too, want no changes made. They worship familiar patterns. New ideas, new methods, new personalities cause them discomfort.

Now is the time to remember the law of the survival of the fittest. We survive or we perish according to our adaptability or unadaptability to our environment.

Each of us must ask: To survive and succeed, what changes must I make in my thinking to fit me to this new environment.

Dear Church worker, know what your neighbors are doing. You visit your neighbors and let them visit you. "From many mouths come good counsel."

When we exchange ideas with one another and are free to accept the best that is within each of us, we are all in a position to have the ideas of all of us "in one can."

"See what your neighbors are doing."

STORY THIRTY-THREE

PYTHON EGGS

When I was a lad, an educator came to Salt Lake and delivered a lecture which he called "Python Eggs." I think it not strange at all that I remember it so well. He reminded us that in India the python takes a toll of thousands of human beings each year. It lays its eggs in the jungle. If the egg hatches, a little demon crawls through the grass and in time becomes as big around as a man's leg. When it matures, it climbs a tree, lies in wait on an overhanging limb, and strangles its victims, as shown by our artist. In destruction of life the only competitor of the python in India is the Bengal tiger.

The native boy in India is taught to keep his eyes wide open for python eggs. When he finds the reptile's egg, he applies his heel and turns. If he doesn't that egg develops into the monster that later devours his pet lamb or goat. Yes, that demon might entwine his own sister or brother. No wonder that when the brown boy has crushed the egg of the python, the jungle echoes a cry of triumph.

By the way, I remember an interesting story of a python: The natives, aware of the powers of this devil of India, were in panic. But his capture, when properly engineered, was easy. This was the plan: In the locality where the python was last seen, a goat was chained to a post. The natives didn't have to wait long—they heard the blat of the poor goat—they rushed to the scene, and there the python was chained to the stake—yes, like a trout that had just swallowed the fly hook; it lay conquered.

The monsters within ourselves that destroy us begin with harmless eggs. If we don't put our heels on them and turn like the boy when he finds the python egg, they destroy us.

Liquor is like the python. Egotism, too, lays its eggs in the jungle. Hatred begins with a small insignificant seed. Selfishness, if not checked, grows big, and lies in wait to destroy us. Dishonesty has its fangs and takes its toll, and if not killed in the shell, wraps itself around us and strangles us to death. Each reptile starts with a seed laid in the grass. Don't let it hatch.

Well do I remember a story told by my mother: The young man is on the scaffold ready to be hanged. Before the noose is put over his head he is given any wish. He asks for his mother—she comes. She goes to embrace him. Instead of kissing her, he bites a piece out of her cheek. Then with all the anguish of his soul he cries out, "Mother, why didn't you teach me when I stole those pencils in school—why didn't you stop me? It went to books, then to horses—now, mother,

I am about to die. Why didn't you teach me?" Yes, taking those pencils was a python egg. The egg was left to hatch.

The drunkard makes his start with just a sip, but that sip is the python egg.

Here's a story I heard told by a girl in Wayne Stake. The story took hold of me: A boy goes to a party. They offer him a cocktail. (It wasn't a fruit cocktail.) He refuses—the gang is determined, but so is he. It is only a thimble full, but he refuses. He is called "panty-waist," "mamma's boy"—but he stands his ground. They tell him he must drink with the crowd and smell like a man. The gang is determined to have him come across. Finally with jaws set, they tell him if he won't be game they will throw him on the floor and put the liquor through his teeth. The boy on the spot rises to the occasion. Like a warrior he faces his foes. He has a secret weapon they didn't dream of—here it is—when he gets through with them, they sizzle.

"Wait a minute," says he, "let's see if you'll put it through my teeth. I want to tell you a story.

"Some years ago a boy was out, as I am tonight. They offered him a drink—he refused. They urged—he weakened and took that night just a thimble full. Next week he took it more readily. After that it had only to be offered him. Boys, he became a drunkard. He fell in love with a beautiful girl. Of course, he straightened up while courting her. He knew she and her family were opposed to drink. They were married. A year later a baby came to town, but by this time the man had gone back to drink. He began to come home drunk. On one of these nights he was challenged by his good wife. She had stood about all she could. In desperation she thundered, 'Bill, you come home again like this, and I'll take the baby and go home to mother!' Well, the demon within him broke loose. He grabbed her arm. It was as if it were held in a vise. He threw her out into the Wyoming blizzard. She grabbed the baby, also an overcoat hanging on a chair by the door. He was so drunk that the second he hit the pillow he was dead to the world. The realization at dawn of what he had done, almost electrocuted him. He came to with terror—he grabbed the door, pretty nearly pulling it off its hinges. He rushed out into the snowdrifts. He was almost a crazy man. One hundred yards from the house he detected a little hill in the snow. With eyes bulging, desperately but cautiously, he dug into the snow. There he uncovered his sweetheart, the mother of his child. She was cold in death. The baby, through the protection of the body of its mother and the overcoat snatched as she left the room, had a spark of life left. The babe was brought back to life."

Defiantly our hero faced the gang. "Now, boys, if you are ready to put that stuff through my teeth I am ready for you. I AM THAT BABY."

The python snake that night crushed the life out of a dear mother. It wrecked the home. If only the demon drink had been crushed in the shell—if a heel had only done its work at the right time! Yes, *it was a python egg.*

STORY THIRTY-FOUR

Mother, have you a boy at home that worries you because of his mannerisms you think sometimes should be more circumspect? Are you worried about him because you think he should be more like a little Lord Fauntleroy in the way he speaks and in the way he carries on at times? Are you worried about his final outcome? Have you at your house a boy that "yelps" like a coyote and "bellows" like a cow? If you are farm folks, have you a boy at your house that gets on his little

Cayuse pony, and jabs his heels into her flanks. As he gives a war whoop passing the house, does he cause you to think the lower regions were let out for recess? Have you one of those fellows that you have to watch eternally or there is an accumulation, a film of some kind, that gradually collects behind his ears? Unless you yourself are eternally on the watch—unless you are eternally vigilant because of his personal "don't-care-ism," is he likely to go to school and disgrace the whole family? (Am I making myself clear?)

We used to have a boy at our house about this particular complexion that I am trying to describe. Would you mind if I told you about him, going somewhat into detail? Let me go ahead.

This particular fellow used to do patrol work in front of his school. I am still not sure whether he was given this particular job to encourage him in face of his depredations or whether he really merited this particular honor bestowed upon him. Well, one day they gave a big show downtown in honor of these fellows who did this particular patrol work for the Salt Lake City schools. Of course, our boy was invited. I mentioned a moment or two ago what would happen on the back of this fellow's neck if eternal vigilance was not playing its part. Well, his mother thought if he was going to this big affair down town he ought to look presentable, and she therefore sent him to the barber shop to be groomed. He therefore went to the hair trimmer and was immediately ushered into the big chair. I suppose his mother had not given too much scrutiny to the personal appearance of her child twenty-four hours previous, and of course all the sins of the family were parading definitely in front of the barber's eyes that day. He asked the boy where he was going, and he told him. With a twinkle in his eye and up to a little mischief, the barber in observing the dirt immediately back of the boy's ear lobes whirled the boy around so that the boy could observe in the mirror the back of his neck. The barber observed with scrutiny: "Well, are niggers invited today?" (Why did the barber ask him that particular question?) Then with the boy himself observing the accumulation back of his ears, the barber pointed to that particular part of his anatomy and asked, "What do you call this?" Please note the boy's quick answer: "Oh," says he, "that's a birthmark."

(You'll note I am trying to describe somewhat in detail the subject of our story. Let's go on with a few more details.)

One night he came home from Primary. (Thank goodness for the boy's honesty.) He told us this story:—I guess he talked too much in Primary. The teacher stood it as long as she could and then had to do something about it. As I got this story, the teacher called his attention to the fact that he was making too much noise and asked him if he hadn't better step out of the class and think things over. He did. Of course as his parent I wanted him to do his part to rectify same. Calling the lad by name I said, "Don't you think we had better go up to the teacher's home tonight and talk things over?" The boy agreed with me and that was our plan for the evening.

Well, I went on with my work in the garden, and pretty soon the sun started to go back over the horizon, and the shades of night began to fall. It was then that I had the shock of my life. I guess the lad thought I had forgotten the call we were to make on his Primary teacher that night. I had a gentle pull at my coat tail reminding me that we were going to make the call.

Now let me pause right here for a moment. When I was a lad and if I had had this experience with my father when I was in Primary, I would have done anything but pray that my father would forget about the visit we were going to make to the teacher with whom we had had some trouble.

Well, to make the story short, we went up that night, and the boy did all the talking, and the teacher gave him another chance. Yes, but in a few days the same thing happened again. Too much talking and the boy was invited again to leave the room to get hold of himself. I was sure the right thing to do again was to visit his teacher. Calling the boy by name I said, "Now you had better go up and see her, and you ask her if she will give you one more chance." He did, and she did. A couple of weeks after, this fellow came home to his mother with this explanation:—(You'll remember I spoke to you about his horse.) He said, "Mother, that's the best Primary teacher in the world." His mother, of course, realizing the trouble he had had with the Primary teacher wondered why such an observation should come from him in the emphatic terms expressed. "Why?" said she. If you are as well acquainted with boys as some of us are, you will know that a lad, with respect to a horse, as far as water and feed are concerned, the horse should live on air. I guess this boy of ours was no exception to the rule. He had staked his horse out in the field, and of course between ball games and marbles he had forgotten that particular day that the animal existed. He said, "You know, Mother, that teacher carried two buckets of water to my horse up in the field." It seemed that the boy had staked the horse out near the home of this particular Primary teacher about whom we are speaking.

May I stop long enough right here to take my hat off, if you please, to that Primary teacher. Notwithstanding the trouble she had with that boy, she followed her real virtues when she went out of her way, on a busy summer day, to carry a bucket of water to a little Cayuse pony, and especially to the pony belonging to the boy who had caused her so much concern in the discipline of her Primary class.

I repeat, "Mother, that's the best teacher in the world."

I am going over the details of this boy's story for definite reasons. Now let's go on with the story.

One day this lad and four other of his pals came to the house dragging behind them, a lame dog. Its front leg was not only broken, but it was also dangling. But the dog was a "thoroughbred." Why in the world were these fellows so interested in a dog so handicapped? Why did their eyes sparkle with enthusiasm as they led the creature back in the yard to an old box, her new kennel? It seemed that the boys had formed a corporation, the total assets of said company being this lame dog. Of course, that dog had to be fed. The finest milk that ever came from a dairy started to pour into that canine's anatomy. Of course the mothers of these boys, including the mother of this boy in question, were up in arms, too—honest-to-goodness milk drawn from cows for babies now being poured into a worthless dog!

You know, it is a strange thing, but boys seem to know much more about animals and biology itself than their mothers give them credit for. This was the case here. Well, at least $5.00 worth of milk had gone into this dog, and the mothers were still up in arms.

Well, you know what the mission of the stork in this work is, don't you? One day the stork started to fly low over the kennel of this new dog in the back yard. To shorten the story, one beautiful morning as we arose we found to our surprise that up in the back of the yard there came yelps from the kennel that told us there was not only one dog, but now there were many. In other words, the corporation had declared a dividend in a "howling" success. Now good cow's milk *had* to be delivered to the back of the yard. Her yelping pups had to have that cow's milk by remote control.

Well, the five pups waxed strong, and in the course of dog nature they were soon half as big as their mother. The time now came to divide the assets of the corporation, and each boy took a dividend, a child of the mother dog. Our boy took his—a beautiful animal like its mother, as beautiful an animal as ever drew a blue ribbon at a fair. It was the pride of the boy's heart. In fact, the whole family was delighted with the animal.

But it was the same old story. An automobile rushing past the house, the auto trying to occupy the same space as the dog, threw the dog to the pavement, and there it lay apparently dead. The boy was home at the time. As big as the pup was and as small as the boy in comparison, notwithstanding this fact, the boy affectionately picked up the animal in his arms and carried it to the kitchen. I said the dog was *apparently* dead. The boy laid the dog gently on the kitchen floor, found an old rug, and placed it over the *apparently* lifeless dog. The subject of this piece rushed into one room and found his sister, another room and found his mother, and then, as it were, this same lad who "bellowed" like a cow and "yelped" like a coyote did everything but force his sister and his mother to their knees with this plea to the heavens: "*That dog ain't going to die.*" If ever there was a sincere prayer that went to the realms above, it was that day in behalf of the injured pup.

The dog got better, it grew to be a real competition to its beautiful mother.

Now what might have happened to that boy if his parents had taken snap judgment against the inward grace of the boy because of some of these outward appearances? I ask you, father and mother, do you think only of the roughness on the outside of a lad or do you unbutton his coat, as it were, and see what kind of a heart beats underneath his jacket? What is your sense of values?

I was attending a big banquet in St. Anthony, about six hundred strong, the select of the land. All the fathers of the stake were there sitting beside their sons. Yes, they hired the biggest hall in the place. Some of us were sitting at the head table. I discovered about three chairs from where I was sitting something that decidedly interested me. It was a half-kept kid. The back of his head looked like the back of a dog. What I'm trying to say is that he'd been neglected. I went on without asking any questions, and yet I got curious. After the party was over, I inquired as to who the lad was. Here is the story I got: Coming down the highway from his home President Hess was accosted by a shabbily dressed lad. The boy was invited to get in the car. He asked, "Where are you going, mister?" The answer was, "I'm going to a party for fathers and their sons." The boy was a real Yankee. He said, "Where is your boy? "I haven't him with me tonight," came the answer of the president. "Well, say, mister, why can't I be your son tonight?" Well, the end of the story is, that urchin sat at the head of the table as big as you please with the rest of us.

Folks, that's America. That's the Church of Jesus Christ of Latter-day Saints. You never can tell what's under that mat of shaggy hair. You can never tell what heart beats buttoned up in that threadbare coat. Let's love him.

I repeat, what are your sense of values? You may have a boy at your home who "howls" like a wolf and "bellows" like a cow, but that same fellow may have deep down in his soul a faith that bursts forth in "*that dog ain't going to die.*"

STORY THIRTY-FIVE

A REG'LAR FIRST-CLASS GUY

A REG'LAR FIRST-CLASS GUY

When you meet a fine young fellow,
Just a robust, careless boy,
And he greets you with "Hello!"
That just thrills your heart with joy,
If to him your friendship's priceless—
Something money cannot buy,
Then you're what he's pleased to label:
"That's a reg'lar first-class guy!"

It has caused me some reflection,
And I've often wondered why
This acme of deep affection:
"That's a reg'lar first-class guy."
Guys fulfill a useful mission;
Guys support, and guys sustain;

Keep erect, maintain position—
Take up slack, and take off strain.

That's the kind of guys we should be—
Guys that steady and sustain;
Guys that serve, support, and strengthen—
Ease the slack, and take the strain.
You have gained the highest title,
When the boys you're passing by
Turn and say to another:
"There's a reg'lar first-class guy!"

Be a guy to some fine fellow;
Show him how to play the game;
Buck him up and keep him level—
Brace him when he's under strain.
Be to him a real companion—
Not too good, and not too wise—
Just a pal, and then YOU'RE LISTED
With his "First Class Reg'lar Guys."

—*David H. Elton*

A few years ago David H. Elton, mayor of Lethbridge wrote the above poem. In spice and value it's a masterpiece.

When the boys you are passing by stop, do they say to one another, "There's a reg'lar first-class guy"?

While it goes without saying, that much delinquency in the world is due to the spoiled child, a great factor in indifference and crime is that we dads and mothers and we who pretend to be responsible for the boys' destiny are not *regular first-class guys*. I mean we don't get his viewpoint, and we are not with him in his amusements. He lives in one world, and we live in another.

Now, there is a difference between being one *with* them and one of them. I knew a school teacher who miserably failed as such because he was one *of* them. He used to slide down the haystack after them. A teacher must maintain his dignity, but he must at the proper time, as it were, "let his hair down" with them in their recreation and fun. Dance with them, skate with them, eat with them, play ball with them, and they warm up to you, and it is then you are in a position to help them.

Two years ago at a stake conference, a bishop came to me and said, "Bishop, there is someone over in the hospital who would like to see you—could you spare the time?" Sure, I had the time. We found lying on a cot a boy fourteen, with a bullet hole straight through his lungs. His life was hanging on a thread. What had caused this catastrophe? Had the boy himself, or someone else, by accident, pulled the trigger? No, that isn't how it happened.

It was Halloween night, and five boys, with the ordinary Halloween boyish pranks in mind, jumped over the farmer's fence to have some fun. The farmer, enraged, came from behind the house with a high-powered rifle. One of the boys had on a white shirt—the farmer took deliberate aim—put the bead on the white shirt and pulled the trigger. That lad lay there as they found him, gasping for breath.

Pardon me if I go on with a few details of this story: The bishop was called in but was told by the doctor that the boy was in too precarious a condition for any visitor. But the bishop—thank God for the virtues of these fellows—with a kindly eye and with faith in heaven's blessings, with a jaw set in righteousness, pleaded, "Doc, if that boy just had an idea that he would get better, if we prayed with him, don't you think that it would help pull him through?" The physician dropped his head and assented, "Bishop, you win, but be as careful as you can."

Well, I have a letter from that boy, and I prize it highly. In that letter the boy told me that for two months the bishop came every night and held his hand. With the help of his Heavenly Father he pulled through.

Now, that was a dastardly deed on the part of the farmer. Of course, they put him behind bars and as I looked upon the limp form of the boy, I had a prayer in my heart that they would *keep* him behind bars.

How many of us put the bead on the white shirt in a boy's recreations and pull the trigger? Yes, and we make him spit blood, and his destiny in life hangs on a thin cord because we lack the proper sympathy. Now, Mr. Dad, do you, and do you, his mother, and do you, his teacher, put the bead on his sports and pull the trigger?

You know we say a lot these days about fishing for boys. Stott who wrote the book *How To Win Boys* emphasizes this matter. Following through with Dr. Stott and his apt comparison as Christ suggested fishing for men—let us keep emphatically in mind that in our fishing we sometimes go with the fish, and we don't give him a jerk. I am not much of a fisherman, but I understand we do some playing with the fish in our efforts to land him, especially when we get on the line a two-pounder that's worth catching! We ought to go more *with* the boy. We ought to be to him a real companion—not *too good, and not too wise—just a pal, and then we are listed with his regular first-class guys!*

"WE ARE JUDGED BY THE COMPANY WE KEEP"

STORY THIRTY-SIX

I believe it was Aesop who tells of a gull that was caught by a farmer, in a trap with some crows. The gull, of course, pleaded his innocence, contending that he was very different from the crows and was not guilty of performing their depredations. You will remember the farmer's reply: "You may be very innocent, but I caught you in this kind of company."

Indeed we are judged by the company we keep. It is true, Christ was found among the winebibbers, but he went there with a definite object in mind, and that was to lift these fellows from the condition they were in. He went there as a missionary of good will. Let's never think our clothes are too nice to be soiled by contacting labor or by those whose apparel is not as good as ours. There is much honesty, integrity, and real value in a calloused hand and in a hand that shows hard work. We are talking here about the fellow who continually associates with and is one of those whose standards he pretends to be above. I am by no means trying to give the impression that wealth in any way means high standards. Sometimes you will find the lowest standards in all the world with those who have money. As one has put it, "Money talks, but sometimes uses awfully bad language." Someone has observed, "You show me his friends, and I'll tell you his real make-up." Again we remind you "*We are judged by the company we keep.*"

For the sake of money or to put ourselves in a higher bracket "socially" do we leave our friends of real integrity and lean towards those who might do us favors? Do you surround yourself with political bacteria that you might pull strings to satisfy your ambitions? When you find those you associate with stooping to do dishonest things, that's the time for you to kiss those fellows good-bye. You see so much of this stuff these days. The air is full of it. I am not talking politics. I did not say a Democrat was honest, and a Republican was not, or vice versa. I am going to keep right out of that.

Years ago a contractor told me a story along this line that I shall never forget. It has its application right here. The artist has pretty well depicted the story as illustrated.

The assets of a rancher were largely his sheep. The old gentleman had three sons, one of whom was supposed to be one of those fellows who was not too bright. The rancher died, and the thing now to do was to divide the estate which, as stated, was largely sheep. The two older boys connived together. They would abide by the wishes of their father before his death, and yet very decidedly they wanted the best of the bargain, and pooled their interests against their simple young brother. As the sheep were to be divided, they thought they would make three pens, putting in each pen a third of the sheep. By the way, this little fellow who was thought not to be too bright had a pet sheep that, like Mary's little lamb, its fleece was white as snow and everywhere the boy went, this lamb was sure to go. He loved it very dearly. He thought so much of it that he decorated it with a blue ribbon. He fondled it and caressed it. Now, the two older boys thought they would capitalize on the love of the boy for the animal. They proceeded accordingly. Into the center pen of these three pens they had constructed, with the dividing of the sheep, they put all the gummers, all the runts, and all the scabby sheep. Of course, they watched that the number was the same in each pen, but into this pen of the culls, they put the pet lamb with the blue ribbon around his neck. Now, it doesn't take much reasoning to follow the philosophy of such a wonderful division of the father's assets. Now, they said to their weak-minded brother, "Willie, you may take your pick." Willie did just exactly what they thought—he made a beeline for the pen wherein bleated the pride of his heart—his pet lamb. He opened the gate, rushed in, put his arms around his pet lamb and said something like this, "My dear little lamb, we have been friends a long while. I have called, and you have come, and because of my affection for you I have put a blue ribbon around your neck. I loved no one of the fold as I loved you, but," he added, "when you get mixed up with a bunch like this, this is where we must say good-bye."

STORY THIRTY-SEVEN

FIX IT OR BURN IT

Do these pictures look familiar?

There is nothing that discredits our Mormon people more than the sights suggested in the pictures accompanying this article. The truth often hurts, but if the shoe fits, let's wear it. Yes, once again, "Let's tell the truth if it kills us." In many villages or towns in the west we are confronted with just such pictures, but the right word to use is "sights." One often wonders how a right thinking individual, the owner of such dilapidated buildings, can live with this picture before him without realizing how these things advertise backwards for him—yes, and for his neighbors. It is a peculiar thing that the same man would never think of going to Church not properly groomed. He would want to put on a clean shirt, and a necktie to match his suit and his shoes. His wife and daughter will come out of that same shack-looking abode dressed "fit to kill." Their new cut of suit and latest style of "peek-a-boo" shoes wage a terrible battle against that tipping-over porch and falling-to-pieces front door. That new pansy Easter hat, what a contrast to that hanging-by-its-eyebrows gate through which the lady of the house walks to her car.

I repeat, what bothers us is this twisted pride we find in some of our people—a self-respect that prompts dress in keeping with our dignity and prestige, and yet an attitude that allows a dilapidated leaning-Tower-of-Pisa cow barn and sheds.

Someone has said, "Clothes don't make the man, but they might just as well advertise for us as against us"; yes, very true, but what about the buildings on our premises. In other words, in plain American English, what is the opinion the stranger is going to have of us and our standards if he is to judge by our falling-away fences and forgotten homes? *Let's fix them or burn them.*

"People seldom buy a house," declared a prominent real estate agent. "They buy an impression." This impression begins with the very first glimpse of the property. Our impression of a city is measured by our first glimpse of her streets, her parks, her lawns, her fences, her business district, and the sanitation around her homes. A well-kept city will do its own advertising.

A story is told of a tourist riding through Utah on the train. He had heard so much of the Mormons that he asked the conductor to please let him know when they came to a Mormon town. Quickly came the reply from the conductor: "Why, we're passing through a Mormon town now." "But," said the stranger, "are those old sheds and fences what the aborigines left as the Mormons came in?"

You know, folks, that's an awful indictment against us, but our stranger friend was in dead earnest. He was serious. If our pride and culture are to be measured by our premises as they are going to be by the clothes we wear, in the name of the pride we are supposed to have, let us make our homes and buildings breathe more of what we stand for. From Mexico to Canada, let us have open season on the falling down house and the "eyesore" cow barn.

Let us ask of each building over which we claim jurisdiction just one question—Is it worth saving? If the answer is no, then tear it down or emblazon the landscape with a good healthy bonfire. *Fix it or burn it.*

House cleaning is as contagious as the measles. Brother member of this Church—and this means you and me—if you live in a town or a village where you have sights such as we are talking about, get out your "Carrie Nation" hatchet and go to work. Make the owner of an unbecoming premise unhappy until he cleans up his place. Perhaps he's been so busy with other problems that he hasn't noticed what you and I see. Teach clean-up in the Primary, preach it in the Mutual, and have your Relief Society get out their "rapid-fire guns." Take this clean-up program to your priesthood quorums, and make life miserable for the fellow who tolerates this negative advertising which doesn't tell what we really stand for.

If we only realized how we appear to others, we would get busy.

Next time we take a ride or a walk, or let's say the next time we go to Church, make a note of this thing we are talking about—but before we get out our hatchet against our neighbor, pull the mote out of our own eyes. Let's ask ourselves, "What should we do to our premises so that they will give the passer-by the right picture of ourselves?" Go from your house to the dog kennel—*fix it or burn it.*

And don't forget another side of this question—real estate values. An old shack will depreciate values of a whole block like a knot in a board. You who have passed through Brigham City the last few years, I ask you, how much do you suppose those beautiful sycamore trees and the parking around them on its prominent streets have added to the intrinsic value of the town? Pardon a guess: The trees and planting cost a thousand or two: they have increased the value of the city property by at least $200,000.

Remember, righteous pride is like charity—it begins at home. Are you in this position relative to your own dooryard—that you have seen the door off its hinges so long you just can't see it? To use a little scripture here in this matter of home upkeep, "We have eyes and see not." Really, down to brass tacks, is there anything in your neighborhood that tells the story told in these photographs? Folks, such relics of apparent indifference and "don't-carism" are perhaps owned by the most cultured and refined people in the world, but what do others think of these people as they ride by? The photographs in this article were taken a few miles from Salt Lake City, and for that matter, could have been taken in the city itself.

Now, 1947 is right upon us. We will be inviting the stranger to our gates. Yes, we want to put our best foot forward, but remember he is going to see us just as we are. We may entertain him, as it were, in our parlors, but he'll pass through our kitchens. We'll show him what we have accomplished, but don't forget for a minute, he'll see what we have neglected. Start now—*fix it or burn it!*

FIX IT OR BURN IT

Oh, look at those buildings all falling down,
They used to be the nicest in town.
Just what has become of your pride that you had?
To glance at this sight, it must have gone bad.
The chimney needs fixing; the roof cries for paint;
The way the porch wobbles would make one turn faint.
The screens are all sagging; the door knobs are gone;
The flowers are dying and look at that lawn!
From basement to attic, it all looks the same.
If the thing's not worth saving, then give it the flame;
Or pull down the shack, the neighbors all spurn it,
But get at it quickly and fix it or burn it.
This world's full of relics, all worn-out and charred,
But why have museums in every back yard?
That there's a great shortage of labor, it's true,
But no one can clean up your place quite like you.
Now Utah is planning a big National Show,
In the year forty-seven, you surely all know;
Let's fix-up and clean-up and burn-up a bit
And make all our homes and our premises fit.
What about the ideals taught us from above
Oh, go a little further than faith, hope, and love?
So let's show the traveler a much better view.
Fix it or burn it—Yes, it means you!

—Marvin O. Ashton

STORY THIRTY-EIGHT

RUNNING LIGHT

The sketch illustrates a story I heard Elder Callis of the Council of the Twelve tell one day as we were sailing through the uppermost parts of the Rocky Mountains going to a stake conference. I think I shall never forget it and its application to us as Church members—or for that matter, to us as citizens of this wonderful land of America. I'm going to tell it the way I remember it and hope Elder Callis doesn't have to correct me in any details.

Down in one of the southern states there had been a bad train wreck. For some reason the details of it had not been received. The engineer pulling his regular load of cars, going on the same track and to the point reported to be the scene of the accident, was instructed to get details and report back.

Up the line fifty or more miles the train with instructions came to the spot of the trouble. There at the side of the track and sprawled on its side lay the steam monster just breathing its last. Just back of it but dismembered from it was the coal car, the only responsibility of our wrecked giant. Just as luck would have it, both the engineer and the fireman of the unfortunate engine had made a successful leap to safety as the locomotive left the track. The two engineers met—the one carrying his regular load of ten to fifteen cars and the unfortunate fellow who must explain things to the management of the railroad.

"Bill, what on earth was the matter?" His fellow engineer had only one answer, "Tom, I guess I was *running light*."

Yes, he had come up the line with full steam on, sixty miles an hour, making the curves at that rate, pulling only a coal car. He was running light.

Germany is now undergoing punishment for her sins. Italy with her selfish dictator has had to bite the ground for her iniquities, and Japan in humiliation is sitting over a fire of strong medicine that she will be swallowing for a generation or two, whether she likes it or not. And we all have a prayer of thanksgiving in our hearts that America, England, and Russia, with their allies, for the sake of civilization and freedom, have been powerful enough to bring the leaders of these offending nations to their knees. The old world again groans a sigh of relief.

But England has some weaknesses to overcome, and Russia, too, doesn't want to gloat too gleefully over her status being too lily-white. Every nation, as it never did before, must take an inventory of herself and correct her shortcomings to save herself from annihilation.

America doesn't want to strut too arrogantly over her successes, ignoring her faults and failings—yes, even if all nations now may be coming to her not only for corn but also for money. Who was it that wrote that story of the proud eagle in its soaring to the top of the highest clouds? With all the pride of an eagle it rested on a high peak. Before it was to soar again, it contemplated on its dominion over the skies and other birds. If I remember the story correctly, during the few moments of resting on that rock a tiny serpent from under the rock crawled up the legs of the bird and fastened itself under the wing of the proud monarch. As it flew again the snake made its attack on the heart of the eagle, and great was the crash that followed.

America has her troubles—as a society of individuals *we are running light*. Too many of us are taking the curves of life going fifty or sixty miles an hour, pulling only a coal car.

The best example of this running light business is the record of divorces. In many of our cities the ratio of separation of husband and wife to their union is one to three. She holds her job, and their home life is reflected in the cabaret and joint at night. Their lives too often are too glorious to be interrupted with the cry of a babe. They would rather run light. They choose to pull only a car. More weight in the way of passenger cars is too burdensome. It would spoil their gay nights with their friends of the same society habits. Children would save many a family wreck if they would be invited to ride.

If I am not making myself clear, let me illustrate the tendency among too many foolish people as follows:

Sometime ago in one of the homes of the elite a marriage was performed. It was a real event. The house was packed with honored guests to see the knot tied. The society of the town, with all the trimmings, was there that night in this palatial home. The minister was bedecked that night with dress and paraphernalia that befitted an occasion so eventful. Two extraordinary families were uniting their offspring. Nothing was left out, in the way of decorations and pomp, that money could buy.

There was just one fly in the ointment. Somebody had brought a year old baby with a daisy pair of lungs. The minister with the open book had just come to the tense moment of the ceremony—the climax of the procedure. "And all through the house not a creature was stirring, not even a mouse." The groom was just about to say the important "yes," and she, too, was getting ready to consent to what they were kneeling about when the air was disturbed with that pair of lungs of that year old cornfed asserting itself. It was like dropping a bomb at a picnic party. Hearing either the young folks or the pastor was out of the question. Consternation and embarrassment reigned supreme.

Well, these embarrassing moments, thank goodness, are not everlasting. The child was taken to the rear, and negotiations were consummated. The ring was put on the proper finger without too much engineering, and they were pronounced husband and wife.

But were there whisperings and gossiping going from mouth to mouth in the confines of that edifice. Indignation at that mother who brought that child was not hidden—resentment crawled right out in the open. Many women cracked their heels on the hardwood floors expressing their resentment at such presumption on the part of the mother.

One young girl about twenty years of age was more vehemently exorcised than any. Her eyes snapped—she stamped her feet. The idea of such conduct! Then she shrieked to her little group of admirers, "You bet your life when I get married I'm going to put right on the invitation 'No Babies Expected.'"

And these days they are generally not expected. Young couples would rather run light.

Members of this Church: Many of the wrecks of life, wrecks that can't be repaired and set up on the track again, are caused because they who suffer are running light.

Let us thank God that we have a load to carry. If we have, we'll take those curves better. Be glad you have your tithing to pay—be glad you are hit with a request to pay on the chapel. These are the things that make men and women of us. Don't ever pity yourself. Pity the fellow that tips over because he won't load himself. Yes, and you'll always find that busybody who won't be magnanimous, trying to cause trouble and suggesting to the loyal how much the latter are imposed upon. These narrow people just go through life with chips on their shoulders.

This Church will be safe as long as we all have loads to carry. This nation will always be in a dangerous position and headed for the rocks when we are trying to run light.

I hope my children and their children's children will keep their feet on the ground. And I know the safest recipe for hugging the rails of life is in carrying a consistent load.

STORY THIRTY-NINE

Breeders of **MEN**

FATHERS OF MEN

You talk of your breed of cattle
And plan for a higher strain;
You double the food of the pasture;
You heap up the measure of grain;
You draw on the wits of the nation;
You better the barn and the pen;
But what are you doing, my brothers,
To better the breed of men?

You boast of your Morgans and Herefords,
Of the worth of a calf or a colt,

And scoff at the scrub and the mongrel
As worthy a fool or a dolt.
You mention the points of your roadster
With many a "wherefore" and "when,"
But, ah, are you counting, my brothers,
The worth of the children of men?
You talk of your roan-colored filly,
Your heifer so shapely and sleek.
No place shall be filled in your stanchions
By stock that's unworthy or weak.
But what of the stock of your household?
Have you wandered beyond your ken?
Oh, what is revealed in the roundup
That brands the daughters of men?
And what of your boy? Have you measured
His needs for a growing year?
Does your mark as his sire, in his features,
Mean less than your brand on a steer?
Thoroughbred—that is your watchword
For stable and pasture and pen,
But what is your word for the homestead?
Answer, you breeders of men.

—Author Unknown

Unwarranted desire for wealth and power intoxicates the human soul. Mr. Father, that precious boy of yours, who is praying for a little of your time, is worth ten thousand times more than that bank account, those stocks and bonds, and that business ambition that you have. Are you too busy to heed him? When you go, those worldly things are of no value to you, but your boy lives after you. He is the monument you leave to your name. Yes, some of you good dads need to be labored with more than the sons. Yes, it is your sheep who have gone astray, not the lambs. It is the biggest wonder in the world that so many of our lambs do go straight.

Some months ago in a stake conference I listened to a splendid talk. After the speaker had finished, the brother sitting at my right nudged me and told me this story: "A year or two ago this man was doing nothing in the Church. All he was thinking about was his business and his club. He very seldom graced the Church. One Sunday morning his twelve-year-old boy, instead of getting dressed for Sunday School, as he always did, continued to read the funnies. The father in surprise said, 'Bill, what's the matter with Sunday School today?' The boy looked his father straight in the face and answered resolutely, 'I am on strike. When you go to Church, I'm going.' Brother Ashton, the answer was a little abrupt, but that was the thing that brought this man back into the Church. That was a wonderful talk he made, wasn't it?"

Once a financially prosperous gentleman was being wheeled off to the cemetery when two acquaintances of the deceased were sitting on the ditch bank whittling away. (You know, these old cronies to whom we sometimes give little ear, do some tall thinking.) As the hearse was moving along with its precious cargo, one of these fellows said to the other, speaking of the deceased, "How much did he leave?" His friend to whom he put the question must have been Irish. Quick as a flash came the reply, "He left everything." Yes, Mr. Father of that boy, when they wheel you away to the graveyard, *you will leave everything*.

A few weeks ago the writer had an unusual experience. He will never forget it. It was anything but pleasant, but this experience has been indelibly impressed on his soul. About four o'clock one afternoon, a very prosperous gentleman came to my office. I would guess he was worth $200,000 or more. He was not a member of our Church, but the writer had done some business with him and had the highest respect in the world for him. He was not a young man, and it seemed that during the past few years, he got the *dollar bug*, or he went money mad. I have learned since this experience that this gentleman would wake up in the middle of the night, call his secretary on the phone to learn the exact amount of accrued interest against a particular loan. He had the dollar so close to his eyes that he couldn't see ahead of it or to the side of it. The day he came to my office, he was terribly worried. While he was a Christian, it seemed the last few years at least, he had given no time to religion. He was too busy chasing the "almighty dollar." He acted as if he could take his accumulation of wealth with him to the great beyond. This day he was worried. He said, "Bishop, some night I want to talk to you. I feel I should be doing something other than worrying and stewing about the things that have been taking most of my attention." He had come to the point where he felt he would like someone to kneel in prayer with him. In the course of the conversation, I told him I thought he should spend his time in some benevolent cause that would call for his wonderful ability to do good.

We made a date, but before the date was consummated—that very night—he put a revolver to his head and took his life. How much did he leave? *He left everything*. What was all that worrying and stewing about wealth worth? Much ado about nothing!

During a recent general conference, President Oscar Kirkham told an amusing experience. Let's use his own words: "Recently at one of our stake conferences one of the leaders of the stake said to me, 'Brother Kirkham, after the morning meetings I wish you would take the opportunity to walk home with my son. I wish you would have a little talk with him. He is not going to his Sabbath school, and I wish you would have a chat with him.' So I looked for the opportunity. I took the chap by the arm, and we started down the street toward the home. I thought a very good approach would be for me to say: 'You know, you have a great father, a fine man,' and so I started out with words like these, and then the boy immediately turned to me and said: 'Brother Kirkham, I wish you would talk to my father for me. In all my life he has never been with me to a movie. He has never taken me with him. I haven't even had a game of checkers with him. I would appreciate your talking to my father.' "

Fathers of men, "Lay not up for yourselves treasures upon earth, where moth and rust doth corrupt, and where thieves break through and steal: But lay up for yourselves treasures in heaven, where neither moth nor rust doth corrupt, and where thieves do not break through nor steal: For where your treasure is, there will your heart be also." (Matthew 6:19-21.)

STORY FORTY

ARE YOU SUSTAINING OR BEING SUSTAINED?

A few years ago on a trip to Canada, along the road we saw the picture accompanying this article. In that particular area of this telephone pole spectacle there had been a flood and a washout. A tidy little stream had come down the mountainside; the telephone pole got in its way; and the water took it off its feet and left it dangling in the air. There was such multiplicity of wires stretching from pole to pole that this unfortunate pole was being sustained in mid-air—the pole was off its feet but held up by the system.

When I saw this I remarked to others in our company, "I guess some of us are just like that pole—we are not carrying a load but being supported by the system. In other words, are you, Mr. Member of this Church, carrying your share of the load or are you just riding? Sometimes we are worse than just riding through the strength of others, and our feet are dragging.

In one of the old books they used to record a story of a Negro minister exhorting his colored congregation to loosen up and half pay the expenses of the church. He was very pointed in his remarks, and really, in his own way, waxed strong in the role of oratory. About at the peak of his plea for funds he challenged his group with, "This church am got to walk."

You know there are generally in each congregation those so emotionally inclined that they automatically echo back when something from the pulpit pleases them. In this meeting there was one of these members present. He was sitting down by the stove with his feet on a chair. When he heard this appeal from his spiritual leader, he groaned back in the spirit of "Glory, Hallelujah. Let 'er walk."

I suppose the minister appreciated this cooperation, but he was only on the first step of his oratorical ascension. He looked his audience in the eye and fired at them, "This church am got to run." Then came the echo from the stove, "Let her run."

Up the scale came the parson with a higher note, "This church am got to fly." It was not surprising when that big voice back in the hall thundered forth, still teaming with his leader, "Let her fly."

Now our minister had arrived at the crucial point in his appeal for help. He had sent out the barrage—had softened the enemy's resistance, and now with fixed bayonet was going to make the attack. Now he was ready to strike to kill. He raised his voice and shaking his fist at those below him fired out, "Now if this church am goin' to fly, you niggers has got to come through with some gold."

Now human nature back by the stove with feet on the chair was going to assert itself. With accent somewhat toned down and not so full of fire he moaned back, "*Let her walk*."

Now, dear member of this Church, if the Church is depending upon you, what is the Church going to do, fly or run? I am not talking of money only, I am talking about the support you are giving this Church. Are you so contented that as far as you are concerned things can just drift? Are you so selfish that as far as any sacrifice you are going to make, the whole thing can just coast along? Do you think more of your money than of the progress of the Church? Are you just indifferent or tight?

Speaking of being tight reminds me of a story of a Scotchman who was being solicited for funds to build a monument in honor of the father of our country. Our friend being approached for help was allergic to such a program if any skin financially was to come from his anatomy. The member of the committee sent to make the contact here was well chosen, but he had a hard nut to crack. Here is the cold draft that chilled our worthy solicitor. (Some of us who have been on drives for the help of good things have had similar experiences.) He whined back at our friend asking for help, "I don't need a monument of Washington to remind me of him. I've got George Washington right here in my heart."

Well, that ball thrown over home plate, swift as from the pitcher's box, was just an opportunity to hit the ball squarely on the nose and knock it over the fence for a home run. Yes, he made a four bagger. Here was his comeback:—"You know, my friend, I'm quite a student of history and particularly American history. I have made a real study of George Washington and his campaigns with the British. I know pretty well how worried he was at times. All I've got to say to you is that if George Washington is in your heart, he's in the tightest place I've ever read of his being in."

I remember years ago out in Sugar House when that little live metropolis was not quite so large as it is now, we went out to get funds to put a big electric sign over the main corner. I think the sign was to read "The Shopping Center." It was to benefit all the merchants. The money was coming in in great style, and the program was going over. Some of us approached a little merchant—I think he was of Israelitish blood. What did he say when we asked him for his support? "Vot is the use—why should I pay? They'll do it anyhow."

Of course we'd do it anyhow. This Church will go forward whether that fellow who rides without paying contributions or not.

Mr. Member of this Church, do you support or do you just hang on?

STORY FORTY-ONE

The more we use an automobile the greater are we awed by what it will do. The phenomenal thing is the engine. No engine, no car! But what makes the engine valuable is the brakes. Under the hood of that one hundred horsepower wonder are two big sisters cooperating with one another—yes, the engine and the brakes, one furnishing the power and the other the controls—neither worth a cent in and of itself but together a combination making one of the miracles of the age.

I said they were sisters—yes, one with her hair down generating power that turns the wheels; the other, fully composed, watching carefully every stroke made by her more aggressive teammate, tempering her ambition with discretion. When this partnership is functioning, no load is too big, and no grade too steep. The engine climbs the mountains, and the brakes make possible the descent from the lofty peaks, helping in a big way to make our civilization what it is. But here's the point: The brakes cannot say to the engine, "I have no need of thee," nor can the engine observe to the brakes that the latter can run its own course without its sister.

Dear Church officer: I don't care what your organization, be you a president of a stake or a bishop, a chairman of a finance committee, or president of a Relief Society or a Primary, that organization is like the automobile—you have therein constituted your helpers, the engines, and you have the brakes. If they are all brakes, you won't climb mountains—you will stand still. If they are all engines without the controls, you will meet disaster, plunging into the mountainside. Some men are engines; some are brakes. Brother head of that organization, don't forget for a minute you need both—one to give forth power, the other to temper its more aggressive brother. Don't surround yourself with all brakes or your destination will be a stagnant pool. Don't surround yourself with only steam and power or your organization will go off on a tangent. Get brakes and get engines, and you'll go somewhere.

A citizen, in speaking to me the other day, was discounting materially a very aggressive member of his community. The fact of the matter is, the man criticizing was the brakes type, the fellow being criticized, the dynamo kind. If we depended upon the first gentleman for life and ginger, we'd all stay in a swamp—yes, and I'll try to be fair—if the man being discounted weren't associated with some of the brakes type he would probably take us off our feet in a whirlwind. Now the fact is, these two men would work well in an organization with a wise leader. They'd go places. Let's encourage the vision, steam, and power, and hold close to us those men who keep us off the rocks where too much enthusiasm would carry us.

In business you need the salesman type who can get the business and keep the wheels of your factory going—yes, but you also need a sound credit department that puts a control on things, scrutinizes the integrity and ability of those to whom you are extending credit. A successfully managed business has at its head one who appreciates the brakes type and the engine type—yes, and who can further instil into its organization an appreciation of one type for the other.

As we paddle upstream, as it were, in the realms of the past, we see clearly the footprints of the giants who have made history and our civilization. Those men who shaped our destiny have been both types—the engine and the brakes type; an Orville Wright breaking forth with genius and exploration, urging us on to fly, and another, a Lincoln, of course, in another realm of steadying civilization with wisdom and inspiration, shaping the rights of men.

History is pretty dim in spots. We don't know very much about this man Gutenberg who gave us printing, but if we read between the lines, he was a genius, and as this type often runs, he had his troubles—not too well balanced in ordinary things of life. If it hadn't been for his good wife who paid the taxes, they'd have had the roof taken from over their heads. He lost his printing presses and all the equipment to the man who lent him money. His death was unnoticed—yet that fellow's genius revolutionized the world.

Columbus died in chains. Pallisy who gave us glazed pottery, in his final experiments tore up the floors of his cottage for fuel, and as his family fled their abode, he threw into the furnace his tables and chairs. Goodyear, who gave us vulcanized rubber and who in a sense revolutionized transportation, made his inventions in jail, confined there because he couldn't pay his debts.

Yes, history proves that the most eccentric ofttimes leavens greatest the whole.

Someone, keeping in mind the value to the world of the honeybee, has said, "Let's pull out the stinger without killing the bee." Now, the Lord has created us differently, with different likes and dislikes, different abilities, different viewpoints, but in the grand scheme of things we all have our place. Let us appreciate the virtues of one another.

In our Church we need the aggressive; we need the conservative. We need the gunpowder, the dynamite, and vitamins in men. We need the engines to climb the heights—we need the brakes to steady our course. We all have our destinies ahead. Let none of us say to the rest of us, "I have no need of thee." If you are the brakes type, appreciate the steam and vigor of others. If you are the engine kind, don't condemn those more cautious. Someone has said wisely of an engine, "It is that which quits pulling when it starts knocking."

I repeat, let us appreciate the great value in men. Some of the most vigorous have to be helped in arriving and departing. Think of the ocean liner, its power, its capacity, its ability to haul men and material across the vast oceans, but don't forget how helpless that huge monster is when it steams into port. It takes the little tiny tugboats to pull it to the wharf to place it for its loadings and unloadings. Some men are like great liners. They have to be helped in and out of some of the details of life. Put them on the high seas where their propellers can function with freedom, and they are giants.

The liner must not say to the tugboat, "I have no need of thee," and the tugboat must appreciate the place in the world of its big sister.

If you are the engine type, don't feel self-sufficient. It you are the brakes type, cultivate companions who look over the horizon seeking new worlds to conquer. We in our Church who are supervisors of men in whatever capacity, let us cultivate these two types with a prayer in our hearts for inspiration from above and help us to place men where they can do the most good. Let us be a little kinder in our attitude towards men who are of different types from us.

STORY FORTY-TWO

ARE YOU USING YOUR HEAD?

It's a sad story, but there are many lads in the world that are not using their heads better than the fellow in this picture. Parents sometimes make every sacrifice in the world for their children, and the response to this kindness is one of the saddest pictures in the world. We sometimes in our thinking come to the conclusion that most of the ingrates are found in the homes of the wealthy. Nothing could be farther from the truth. Some of the most outstanding examples of stupid ingratitude are found in the homes of the poor or the homes of those struggling to maintain themselves.

Let me tell you the story as illustrated. A good brother with a twinkle in his eye told it to me in a little huddle in the interest of young people at a meeting we had a year or so ago in Nephi. If you have a funny bone of any size at all in your make-up, you'll get a tingle out of it.

The subject of our interest in the picture is a boy of about sixteen. I guess he'd never made much money himself. The family lived out there on the fringe where money didn't flow too easily. As I got the story, the lad didn't know what a "greenback" looked like except by remote control. As simple as their lives were in this family, every sacrifice had been made for him. Mother had skimped and gone without things to favor her son. The patches on his clothes were just a reminder of a scanty family budget. One item of the boy's welfare that was unselfishly catered to was his education. The head of the household let his affection for his offspring decidedly flood over and encompass better judgment. What I am trying to say is that the father would have been wiser if he had been more interested in the boy's appreciation of what was being done for him and had less disregard that he himself gave to the callouses on his hands, put there through love for his own flesh and blood.

Well, in a moment of family financial worries the State Road Commission came to their neighborhood with a little unexpected work. It was at a time when the wolf was doing a little howling at their door. The boy got about ten days work. How the family watched the day when their son would be walking home with that pay envelope. They had done everything but go hungry, and now that cash, as little as it was, would replenish their cupboard. It would get a few things they just needed to keep their bodies and souls together.

Pay day came. The lad actually came down the street with $16.00 in his pocket. The money was like a gold mine, and this day was the biggest holiday in his life. He strutted down the little village store street like a victorious game rooster. The world was his. He now jingled the stuff that would buy things he wanted in his Levi pocket.

He didn't get very far. A pair of riding boots in a show window, trimmed with red, stopped his heart from beating. Gosh, he'd wanted something like those for years. He found the price to be $16.00. He must have had Israelitish blood in his veins, for in about as short a time as it takes to tell it he marched out of that store proudly parading those boots. The flashes of his pride dazzled the eyes two blocks away. He strode towards home. Mother and dad of course were watching the clock when that money would arrive.

His father saw red up the street first. He rushed to the gate. While the son walked the block left between himself and home, his good dad had enough time to calm himself and comb down the bristles of his anger. The two met just outside the gate—the eyes of the hard-working father were riveted on the new boots trimmed in red.

"What have you been doing, John?"

"Buying a pair of boots, Dad."

"What did they cost, John?"

"Sixteen dollars, Dad."

"But that's all you had, wasn't it, John?"

"Yes, Dad."

The head of the house pulled himself together again, counted to ten, scratched his head, took a step back—himself now under full control. He took a good look again at the fancy trimmings on the boots. He let his eyes travel up the lad's repaired over-and-over-again clothing and finally came to a full stop at his son's sheepish eyes. Then came a bullet—not a blast, but a direct shot with the power of a French thirty.

"That's all right, John. You take care of your feet. Your head's doing you no good."

You know, that kid that day wasn't using his head. I suppose the father learned a lesson, too, that day that shaped the future tutorage of their son. I wonder if up to that day about all the footprints of kindness hadn't gone in only one direction—from the parents to the child.

Fathers and mothers, before it's too late have that boy or girl do something for you.

Dale Carnegie in his book *How To Win Friends and Influence People* says if you want to make a friend of the other fellow let him do something for *you*. Yes, and it works the same in raising boys and girls. If you want them to love and respect you, let them from the time they crawl sacrifice for *you*.

If you want your children to turn and rend you, just keep taking the skin off your hands for them and demand nothing in return.

While I am saying this, a panorama comes before my mind of a merchant I once knew. He was one of the highest type men I ever knew. He was loved by all who did business with him—he had a keen mind and was a real thoroughbred. He could have been mayor of Salt Lake City he was held in such high esteem. But he had one weakness—one fly in the ointment—he was too good to his children. He sent his boy off to school, gave him everything but his checkbook with all the checks signed in blank. If the boy wanted anything, all he had to do was to wiggle his little finger, and the father would come trotting in his direction. He asked for no consideration from his children, and he got none. I think the father was worth probably a half million, but by the time that son got through taking his father for financial rides, there was hardly, I think, enough money left to put his father's remains in a box to go under six feet of ground.

And that isn't all. That boy would talk to his father as though he were talking to a dog. He would do everything but order him about. What happened to the son ultimately? I don't know. Some years ago he had already been divorced a couple of times and left a trail behind him that, to put it lightly, would make your heart ache. He was nothing but a spoiled, "lopsidedly" educated ingrate.

I intimated that not all the spoiled children were brooded in the homes of the wealthy. Some of the most helpless boys and girls come from humble cottages where fathers and mothers slave for their children. One of the most helpless young men I ever knew passed on to a next generation was from the family of a hard working school janitor. I loved him and his good wife, but their offspring were never taught to do something for dad and mother. They were *bottle babies* until late in their teens.

But I repeat, have your children do things for themselves and also for you. Then you'll pass on to the next generation something worth keeping.

Fathers and mothers, be wise. Sons and daughters, use your heads.

STORY FORTY-THREE

YOUNG MAN . . . DO YOUR OWN THINKING

AT THE CROSSROADS

You'll stand at the crossroads all alone,
The sunrise in your face;
You'll have to think, for the world's unknown,
 And set your jaw for a manly race.
Yes, the road goes east, and the road goes west.
Young man, you'll have to know which is best.
One road ahead, my boy, will lead you down.
And you can lose the race and a victor's crown.
Don't get caught in an angry snare
Because alone you stood at the crossroads there.
Know *yourself* the better way.
Stand alone at the crossroad place
 As a boy of high hopes would;
With your face all set for a manly race.
 With your chin to the sun, seek the things that are good.
As you stand there alone, the road you must know,
The only one on which to go.
Turn from the road that leads one down.
You'll win the race and the victor's crown.
You'll walk today the highway fair,
Because *you yourself* were set at the crossroads there.
To choose you the better road.
(Paraphrased by Marvin O. Ashton)

Young man, the important thing after all is, can you stand all alone or do you have to be propped up,—or, putting it a little stronger, are you in good company when you're alone? Can you paddle your own canoe? It's a mighty fine thing for you to contemplate having someone with you always to show you the better way, but life just can't be that way. The big-

SUCCESS
FAILURE

gest part of the time no one can be there to point the way for you. Can you go through life on your own steam? No matter how the tempest rages around you, can you choose your course?

> One ship drives east and another drives west
> With the self-same winds that blow,
> 'Tis the set of the sails and not the gales
> Which tells us the way to go.
> —Ella Wheeler Wilcox

At the time you will make great decisions, that father and mother and those who have helped you in the course before may be hundreds of miles away. It's the stand you take then that will determine your destiny. When temptation sticks up its hideous head and beckons you on, will you have the courage to say "no"?

Here's a little story that I hope will thrill you as it did me:

A president of a certain stake in our Church buys and sells cattle and sheep. He goes east very often to sell. He has a son that he sometimes takes to Chicago with him. This particular fellow, besides having a mind of his own, has a sense of humor—I mean, he is blessed with a comeback. Well, we're talking now about a certain trip the father made when he took this young man with him. At one time the cattle salesman was called unexpectedly to another town, and the boy was left alone in Chicago in care of the men who habitually bought his father's cattle. Now, part of the program in going east to sell is the entertainment of the buyers. These buyers, knowing the shipper was called away, were doubly determined to spare no means in giving the boy a royal reception. They must take him to the most elite clubhouse in the city. The young man was to receive club hospitality and all the trimmings, and they proceeded accordingly.

The first step towards up-to-date hospitality in a place like he was ushered into is the cocktail bar. It's a place where you are served a cocktail before the meal, and it isn't a fruit cocktail. They had already offered the lad the cigarets, and he had refused. Now came the drink. It was offered him on a shining silver tray. It beckoned him on with all the enticement in the world. As it was offered to him, the boy shook his head. The buyer leading the party, with a mixture of surprise and disgust, made up his mind to put this "panty-waist" sissy from Mormondom in his place. Others were huddled around, and it was really, in a small way, a fine place to make a grandstand play at the expense of the lad from the west. With a sarcastic grin and a determination to humiliate, he shot out at the boy, "The telephone is right there—would you like to call your mother long distance and ask her if she'd give her consent for you to drink with us?"

Well, that was enough to take the starch out of some fellows, wasn't it? But not this lad. I said he had a little Irish blood in his veins. Looking his smart-aleck host steadily in the eye, under full control, he gently countered with, "My mother thinks that tonight I'm out with gentlemen."

> You are the handicap you must face.
> You are the one who must choose your place.
> You must say where you want to go,
> How much you will study the truth to know.
> God has equipped you for life, but he
> Lets you decide what you want to be.

Someone has wisely said, "A fellow with the right kind of stuff in him preaches to himself harder than anyone else can." And someone else said, "A wise man is like a straight pin—his head keeps him from going too far."

Young man, a thousand miles away from home, can you keep the standards of your mother and father? One man changed the history of the world by taking into a foreign country these standards: He was good looking; he had personality; he was young. Because of his physique and general carriage, he carried prestige. She was a woman of importance —yes, I presume she was attractive. She tempted him once— she tempted him twice—yes, and many more times. Each time he remembered the teachings of his folk at home. He looked sin in the face and stood like a rock. Yes, as the saying goes, he took it on the chin.

For just a moment what a price he paid to keep straight— and don't forget he was praying all the time. When she found herself unvictorious, she caught his garment as he fled. The sample of the clothing was shown to her husband, and if we can use our imagination, a remark from her treacherous lips went to her husband about as follows: "Well, here's the evidence. You thought he was lily-white, didn't you?" Into a dark dungeon he went for two years. And he was still praying. And when he was sold into Egypt by his brothers for a few pieces of silver, he was praying. Does the Lord really answer prayers?

But let's shift to the last act of our play. The curtain goes up with an entirely different scene, "And they came from all nations to buy corn." Who was head of this great commissary department? Who was it that was next to the king of the land? Joseph who was sold into Egypt, the boy who could say "no"—the lad who took the standards of his parents into a foreign land! It was that boy who stood at the crossroads all alone. That youth, the day when he told the woman, as it were, "Get behind me, Satan," changed the history of the world. If you, dear reader, can think of the history of Israel without seeing Joseph sold into Egypt, a central figure, you can do more than I. You can't think of the history of the world without seeing Joseph with a coat of many colors playing a major role.

We all come almost daily to the crossroads in our lives where we make decisions. Let us "not be caught in an angry snare, but walk today on the highway fair."

STORY FORTY-FOUR

HE'S A THOROUGHBRED

Yes, he's a thoroughbred. They've kept water away from him for three days and then let him loose. He was so thirsty he'd have eaten mud, but he's passing up the gushing spring and makes a beeline for his master's tent. Look at his extended nostrils — observe that intelligent head. He's an Arabian thoroughbred.

Let me tell you the story:—A good bishop told it at a boy's leadership meeting. I hope it thrills you as it did me:—

They tell me that all fleet-of-foot horses that have made a name for themselves have originated from that old Arabian stock. I am talking about race track history and horses with their generals who have made history. We bear in mind that this is the grandfather of them all, the Arabian blood. The Arab thought as much of his mount as he did of his children. These animals were watched and tutored better than their children. The horse through the ages has been the best friend of man, and these Arabs in developing this great creature "builded better than they knew." The horse was the pride of the family, and his development was watched and guided with the greatest love in the world.

Well, let's get on with our story. Now let's note one thing about this animal's training. They determined that he should in very deed be a thoroughbred. When the colt is a few months old, they ring a bell and push the little fellow over to his master's tent. To make the story short, they repeat that operation until in a few weeks the intelligent fellow automatically, when he hears the bell ring, turns right about, no matter what he is doing and trots off to his master's headquarters.

But the day of testing is coming—a day, if you please, when his mettle will be tried—a test to determine whether they've raised fifteen hundred pounds of horseflesh or a creature to be labeled a "thoroughbred." Well, just what do they do with him; how do they determine his worth? Now watch —here are the details of the examination: He's now going to get a diploma or be labeled a cull.

The horse is now about three years old. They have rung this bell every day, and he hasn't missed a perfect response—not a hesitation at the sound of the gong, a beeline to the tent of his master. But so far no great sacrifice has been asked of him, but on this day of exam it's going to be different. They keep him, as I said, away from water for three days—his tongue is as thick as leather. That third day he's done everything but jump over the fence to water. While in this desperate condition, when everything is ready, they let down the bars of the corral. He leaps like a deer—when he's half way to water, they ring the bell. If he continues his run for water, he's a cull. If he turns right about to his master's tent, he's a thoroughbred, and he is sent over the ocean and to the ends of the earth, as may be demanded, for breeding purposes.

The progeny of this fellow have given the world the horse

ridden by George Washington in his campaign and the black charger that old Phil Sheridan rode that famous day from Winchester to the battle twenty miles away.

That day that desert charger forgot his thirst—he forgot himself—he was intent on only one thing—service to his master. As fleet of foot as only an Arabian beauty can "cut the wind," he charged across the open spaces to do his duty.

Young man, are you a cull or are you a thoroughbred? That is the question. Young man, are you letting your appetites run you or are you thinking of your duty? In plain American English, do you hear the bell ring or are you bent only on responding to your desires?

Men who make history are men who have governed their appetites. Young man, the eyes of the world are on you as they never were before. Probably there never was a time when there has been a greater letdown in control. Pray to the Lord eternally that he will bless you with energy, bless you with vitamins and spunk to carry on. When you say your prayers at night ask him to give you, if you please, a reservoir of vitality and ambition to fight the battles of life, but ask him to help you govern yourself.

Look at that panting, throbbing steam engine. There is enough steam in that huge boiler to blow the monster itself over the moon. But see how it's organized—every valve and every jet cooperating together to pull those fifty cars over the Rocky Mountains. And that's exactly what it can do and does every day. Just with the beck and call of the engineer's little finger, as it were, that giant rises to its feet, stretches its limbs and speeds across the continent like greased lightning—the Iron Horse, under full control of his powers. Like the Arabian steed it hears the gong and is at our tent to do our bidding.

Young man, be a thoroughbred.

STORY FORTY-FIVE

Under Full Control!

Yes, this is the same horse. Let me tell you about him.

A few months ago my doctor neighbor said to me, "Bishop, there's a daisy horse show in Kaysville tonight. Let's go." We went out. It wasn't a horse race. It was a show where these beautiful animals were shown off. Whenever you get a chance to see a good horse show, be there. I forget most of what took place that night except the act one particular horse gave us. She was a beautiful bay creature. A good-sized man would have to stand on tiptoes to reach the top of her magnificent head. She really looked the part—man's greatest friend.

They then threw off the saddle and put her between a pair of shafts, drawing what they call a sulky. This is no more than a toy four-wheeled pneumatic-tired buggy. The vehicle was so light a lad could throw the whole thing over his shoulder. (I'm exaggerating, but I'm enjoying it.)

They first put a saddle on her and just with a little gentle coaching from the rider she went into the five gaits. She walked, she trotted, she paced, she did the single foot, and then off with a gallop she went. But this feat didn't inspire me too much—I'd seen that done before.

The driver got into the seat made for one only, tightened up the reins, and away she charged around that track. Every eye in that crowded grandstand was riveted on that parcel of dynamite plunging around the disk. You could pretty nearly see from the grandstand those big veins that led to her aristocratic nostrils. If ever there was a display in horseflesh, of gunpowder, and ginger, it was in that animal as she split the air showing her speed to the crowd. Her front feet hit the terra firma as if it was the last stroke she was going to make on this earth. What a sight—it animated everyone. As she was in the height of her glory showing us what she could do, my doctor friend poked me in the ribs and the following broke forth from his animation: "If the Lord made only a horse! Every stroke she makes shouts to the world there is a God—there is a Creator." Those leather veins were as though they were steel. It seemed such a force was pulling them from her bit that if she had been attached to a thirty ton car of coal her determined yet sensitive mouth would have drawn the load.

Up to this point I am trying to picture a thrill of five thousand people. But you haven't seen anything. As the crowd sat spellbound, something happened with that horse and buggy that brought everyone in the grandstand to his feet—an accident! Just as that horse hit that northwest curve, the speed of the turn was too much for that toy vehicle—too great a burden on that flimsy wheel. It crumbled like a peanut shell.

What's going to happen to those people in the wake of that pair of shafts holding that piece of T.N.T. animal explosive? (By the way, I have seen what runaway shafts will do. I have seen them make a hole in an oncoming horse a foot and a half deep.) I said everyone arose as if he had been pushed up automatically by the earth itself below.

Well, what did happen? The driver rolled out of the buggy—we expected that—nothing else could have been expected. But they say sometimes a horse in a runaway becomes blind—is oblivious as to what he's doing. Not that horse that night—as that wheel crashed, she stopped like a cow. All that gunpowder we have been talking about became a limp lump—as I said what a moment before was a meteor now was a relaxed cow ready to be milked.

The spectators too relaxed—gave their applause. Why had she so got hold of herself—why such control? *She was a thoroughbred.*

I wouldn't give ten cents for a boy that won't wriggle—a boy that hasn't in his system a bunch of nitroglycerin. But I like to see him wriggle at the right time. A colt that won't kick up her heels won't break many records on the race track. *We are talking about control.*

Under the hood of every healthy auto are one hundred horses playing with the bit—just ready for its master to say, "Get up." Gasoline is twenty times as powerful as dynamite. (I saw a Salt Lake City fireman take a sponge half as big as your fist, dip it in gasoline, and then squeeze the daylights out of it—all that was left in the sponge was odor, and that gasoline-perfumed sponge after being put into a doll house, when electrically ignited, blew the house into oblivion.) There is enough gas in the tank of any one of those normal autos to blow that car a few feet this side of Mars—but do you hear of a car exploding? I don't know that I have ever heard of such a catastrophe—but why? Because it is under control. A good driver, because of the control features of an automobile, will do everything but drive up to an egg and touch it without breaking it. (I believe our friend Ab Jenkins will come next to doing that.) We are talking about control.

A couple of years ago the sin of a young man was brought before the First Presidency. I will never forget the occasion—I am still thinking of the suffering of that fellow's beloved mother when the news had to be broken to her. The unfortunate fellow (and he was unfortunate—someone has aptly said, "To be weak is a catastrophe") had to be handled for his fellowship. It was serious business. I will never forget the observation of President Clark. These were his exact words as I remember them: "Brother Ashton, the trouble with this kind of fellow, ofttimes, is that he thinks he is the only person in the world that has human nature."

Every mature man or woman has natural biological urges—that's human nature. Am I getting too frank? The important thing with all of us is, are we under control?

Dear member of this Church, dear citizen of this great country, are you under control? To the right of you, to the left of you, behind and in front of you, you see the ruins as a result of lack of control. We see broken homes and love scattered like fallen glass all about us because both men and women, boys and girls are not under control.

Let's be thoroughbreds.

STORY FORTY-SIX

POLL PARROTS OR THINKERS?

I make no apology whatever in repeating again the observation of a young man of our Church some months ago. When called on to give a talk in a ward sacrament meeting, he relaxed and told the congregation the innermost workings of his mind. Said he, "When one of our family is to give a talk, Pa writes it; Ma corrects it; and my brother Bill runs it off on the typewriter. Tonight I'm going to say just what I feel."

I have a copy of that talk, and it is an inspiration. It takes hold of you and does something to you. It stirs you.

With all the good intention in the world, that father and mother were on the road to make of that boy and others in the family poll parrots, machines repeating what someone else had thought out. Your arm is made to do things by using it. Strap it down for only twenty-four hours without giving it a chance to operate and see what happens. The mind working through the brain acts accordingly. Think today, and you think more easily tomorrow. Do you parents want to make of your boy an individual or an echo—a generator of thought or a phonograph? I repeat, do you want him to function as a child of God, an individual all of himself, standing on his own feet, or a weather vane whose destiny is shaped by the action of the wind?

I am expressing myself rather emphatically because of what I see in going from stake to stake. Time and time again in going to a stake conference I have seen everyone on the program reading his talk. Sometimes, I must confess, when those talks have been read they have been of the boy's own composition, but invariably he is functioning as a parrot glibly unreeling a line of somebody else's language—yes, using words that pretty nearly strangle his anatomy. This tendency is really alarming. Of course, when he reads it well, it goes over smoothly; but in following a program of this kind, what are we doing to the boy? I would rather my boy hesitated and flickered and sputtered and blasted his innermost workings for the right words rather than to make of him a talking machine. It will be hard at first to make his talk his own, but it will develop will power, self-expression, and in the long run, self-reliance. Reversing the operation, let him lean on someone else's thought the first time, and he'll lean again, and, yes, he'll keep leaning. One of the most sacred things about any of us is our thinking things through and standing on our own feet.

Probably the Church has not developed many greater thinkers than B. H. Roberts. Our Church bookshelves are spotted with his books—textbooks and histories. His discourses are masterpieces. It is said that when he made his maiden speech in school, the attempt was such an effort that his listeners laughed him down. But he wasn't licked—that arm came up; and pointing to those schoolmates, he accepted their challenge. He thundered back, "Some day you'll listen to me." And they did.

The story of Demosthenes of Greece is an inspiration. Yes, his first attempts as an orator were crude and very ineffective—yes, they were failures. His failures were his challenges. Several things bothered him when he arose to express himself before his fellows: First, the crowds before him made him self-conscious—they bewildered him; second, he stood before his audience awkwardly; in particular, one shoulder was much higher than the other; third, he had an impediment in his speech; fourth, he knew if he was to be an orator he must study hard and long; and he realized, too, that he liked to go out at night — he was decidedly a social being, but self-denial must step in here or he would be a failure.

Well, what did he do to overcome these obstacles? To overcome his first trouble, he went out and rehearsed his sermons to the ocean waves as they roared over the rocks. His second trouble—he gave his orations in a shed standing below two suspended swords hanging one over each shoulder. If one shoulder went a little higher than it should, the sharp point of the sword was a gentle reminder. To overcome his speech impediment he put pebbles in his mouth—he said to himself: "If I can give my speeches with pebbles in my mouth, I certainly can talk with ease when the pebbles are out." Now to top off his self-education, so that he wouldn't go out at night, he shaved just half of his beard. (Of course that would keep any man home at night.)

But when this fellow Demosthenes was through with himself, all Greece listened to him. When some other men "orated," people said they were remarkable. When Demosthenes spoke, he put such fire into their souls that they went out and subdued their enemies. When Demosthenes spoke, all Greece arose. Probably the world has not produced a greater orator than this fellow, and yet I remind you again of what an unpretentious start he made.

We are encouraging the reading of too many speeches among young people. Yes, I'll agree with you that you are putting out a more nearly perfect specimen of English composition when they are read, but what *if* every "i" is dotted, so to speak, and every "t" is crossed, what about it? What is a talk for? It is to stir us, not to show how well one can put things together. Someone has said that the English language should be used to express thought, but often it is used instead of thought.

I want to make myself clear: Our conventions and meetings of like nature are programed with too many written talks. Very often if the audience didn't have manners and were not as thoughtful as they should be for the fellow reading the manuscript, they would groan in unison when they see him unroll his frozen discourse. I repeat again, what is a talk for? It is to stimulate! Written talks as a rule do not stimulate—we tolerate them. If we who listen would be more kind and less critical, people, who are put on the program to guide our thoughts, would feel more at ease and would give us more to think about. When the speaker is before us, we want to see his eyes sparkle and his countenance send a message along with what he says. I repeat again, the test for a talk is not in how does it *look* in print, but what does it *do* to us?

Let's teach our children to talk to us, not at us. When they appear before us, let's encourage them to be themselves, and of course their better selves. Let us encourage them to read much, converse much, study all angles of what they are going to present, seek in every way to get the best thought—yes, and, if necessary, make note to guide consistently and thoroughly what they're going to say. We want to be stirred by the spirit.

Good sense dictates that there are occasions when a talk should be given word for word. This is especially the case in most talks over the radio. Many official instructions from the leaders of our Church and nation must be constructed carefully and given verbatim. In these observations I am keeping these occasions in mind, but I am emphatic in saying we are overdoing it. We are frightening people to death in our expecting perfection—we are driving too many to read talks because we are not more kind. ". . . The letter killeth, but the spirit giveth life." Let us have more life.

I shall never forget a twelve-year-old deacon giving a talk some time ago in a stake conference. He started off at a good clip, but halfway through he stopped. He was like the fellow who was stuck with nothing to unload. Well, it sounded as if Pa wrote it; Ma corrected it; and Bill ran it off on the typewriter. Some of those words were just too big for his tongue. He hesitated—he turned red—the poor little fellow was embarrassed to death. I sat immediately behind him—I could touch him. Seeing his predicament, I finally pulled his sleeve, and I said to him, "Young man, wouldn't you like to tell us right from the shoulder what is in your heart?" He straightened up, put his chin to the sun; fear left him. Then words came to him like fresh water from a spring. Not every man there had his handkerchief out, but that boy that morning "melted" the priesthood of that stake.

May heaven's blessings ever be with the boy or girl who makes such humble beginnings.

Let us not raise parrots—let us, with the inspiration from our Heavenly Father, develop devout thinkers.

STORY FORTY-SEVEN

"OH, WHAT SHALL THE HARVEST BE?"

It is probably correctly observed that one of the biggest and yet the saddest crops in America is the "spoiled child."

You can see by a glance at the illustration who "rules the roost" in this home. Yes, he holds the scepter in thousands of

American homes. Yes, you'd like five minutes alone to handle this selfish little piece of humanity. May I observe here that it is not always the fault of his father and mother, but of others who take a hand in making his bed too much one of roses. Someone has said, "The reason there are so many spoiled children in America is that you can't spank grandmothers." I say you'd like to handle this fellow. What resentment flashes through your mind? You recall the comments of some wise old owl who said, "There's nothing in life more important than a slap on the back, but it should be administered young enough, often enough, and low enough." "We are God's children but not his darlings." I am not too much a convert to corporal punishment, but you certainly see some sad pictures where an occasional application has been neglected.

In a year or two this piece of parent-made selfish anatomy will be taken to school. If the mother hasn't repented of her indulgence, she will take her offspring by the hand, offer him gently to the teacher in charge, with instructions like this: "Wilbur has been brought up rather sensitively. Miss Smith, spank the boy next to Wilbur—let him see you do it; it will do him good."

But what this child needs really is not any punishment vicariously—not by remote control, but by direct application. I am not an advocate of bodily punishment, and I will go further and say that probably the best citizen never had a hand laid on him. Correction has come in some other way. But when selfishness has been developed in some children whom you see about you, your impulses seem to cry aloud for some treatment that will jar this creature into consistency.

Mothers who raise the child by the book
Can, if sufficiently vexed,
Hasten results by applying the book
As well as applying the text.

A child who never feels will never be a leader. A child who has not been taught to make some sacrifice will never know what others suffer. He should be taught to think of others while he is in the "gristle stage," before his bones get set.

There is a story of a stranger seeing a child of six carrying a buxom corn-fed child of two. The tourist was concerned over the weight of the load being carried and the size of the little creature doing the carrying. She observed, "Isn't that a heavy load for you to carry?" Then came the cheerful reply, "No, he isn't heavy; he's my brother." Now, that child was taught in the home "bear ye one another's burdens."

Teach your children from the start to share with others. That's what makes character. That's what makes people delightsome. Some years ago, I believe it was in London, a "Sympathy School" was established, a school to teach youth sympathy for others. To bring these lessons vividly home to the student, sometimes one leg was tied up for the greater part of the day so the pupil would know how it felt to be lame. One day a bandage was tied over his eyes so he would know what it meant to be blind.

If you, Mr. Dad, give a young boy all the spending money he needs without any effort on his part, he won't do any sweating. A friend of mine went out in the country for berries. The fruitgrower whom he called upon said he had plenty of berries but no one to pick them. A lad, about twelve years old, heard the conversation. Said my friend to the boy, "Would you like to earn a little money picking fruit?" The answer came: "No, sir, Dad gives me seven dollars a week spending money, and that's all I need, I don't want to pick berries."

The other night I called to a son of my neighbor, "Bill,

how would you like to work for me a couple of hours?" I didn't have to wait a second for the answer. "Nope."

"Why?" said I. He came back at me, "Dad *gave* me a dollar."

Does your son stand on his own feet? In your home, dear dad and mother, do all the footprints of kindness show in one direction—from you to your boy or girl? See to it that the footprints of kindness show from them to you.

Lincoln at ten was so schooled in sympathy and devotion for others that at this age, a year after the passing away of his darling mother, he arranged for a passing minister to come and give a prayer over his mother's grave.

About a year ago in coming from Los Angeles on the train, I sat in the diner opposite a lady with a pair of spoiled sons, one about ten, the other about seven. Before the meal was over, I was sorry those boys showed up in company as they did, but she was only sitting in the nest she had made for herself. Meat was hard to get. Nevertheless, somehow beefsteak was on the menu. The waiter first brought a big juicy Swiss steak and placed it in front of the younger son. I suppose it cost the mother at least two dollars. You'd think the lad would have jumped over the moon to put his teeth into that wholesome meat. But he pouted, bringing his nose as close as possible to his forehead. His attitude told about this story: "Ma, give me five dollars, and I'll eat it." In came the second steak, and it was presented to the boy ten. Yes, he showed his home training, too. (I should say lack of training.) His nose went up too, as much as to say, "Ma, pay me ten dollars, and I'll eat mine." Well, they carried on. The mother would have liked to crawl in a hole. I wouldn't have been surprised if she had been capable that moment of almost wishing she had no sons. With a flushed face she turned to me and said, "Oh, these American children." I didn't answer her according to my observations, (I've got enough to answer for), but I said to myself, almost aloud, "Yes, and, oh, some of you American mothers."

Now that boy ten and his brother were "boobs," and they are going to grow up men who are "boobs."

Now let's suppose that ten-year-old "boob" in ten or twelve years more of pampering falls in love with a girl under-privileged (and I use that word very carefully) the same way. They marry—I ask you, dear reader what kind of load of responsibility in the way of offspring will they hand on to the next generation? What is the name of that Sunday School song?—Oh, yes—"*Oh, What Shall the Harvest Be?*"

Yes, this nursing should stop. This calf is old enough now to be rustling for itself. Some children in the same way are "nursed" long after they should be weened. The accompanying picture is prompted by my boyhood experience: We

had a big family at our house and we always had to have a cow. Milk and plenty of it was a big item in budgeting the family commissary. Of course a necessary item in having plenty of milk is that a calf must arrive at regular intervals. Calves were such a nuisance that it was to be expected that

Father bargained with the butcher about once a year to come and buy the new offspring.

But in all well-governed homes there are exceptions to the rule. How well I remember the exception: The stork one bright morning brought a beautiful little jersey heifer. She was a beauty. Father, too, fell in love with her. No butcher was called, even six weeks after Bossie's confinement. That attractive little girl was going to reach womanhood no matter at what barnyard inconvenience.

The calf waxed strong and was now six months old—old enough to be on its own, but the animal persisted in drawing its livelihood from the milk headquarters. Something had to be done. The mother cow was perfectly willing to continue the indulgence of her child.

Well, one day Father came home with a halter for that calf—the strangest piece of harness I'd ever seen, the strap that fit over the nose inlaid with protruding spikes. It doesn't take much intelligence to understand why the little heifer would now be kept from the milk headquarters. Imagine the surprise of that cow after nursing a child the night before to find that it had next morning joined the porcupine family. You can see how poor Bossie would get the worst of it.

You know, for years I thought of the injustice of that halter with the spikes, worn by that heifer calf. Why should the parent suffer—why didn't Father bring home a big strap with spikes, to fit around the hindquarters of the cow so the offender, the calf, would suffer? But the older I get, the more sure I am that Father's philosophy was right, that the parent should get the worst of it. You can see how well our cartoonist has shown that the dear cow is reminded that "*the nursing must stop.*"

Dear parents, the greatest gift you can pass on to the next generation is to hand to it a citizen that has been taught to paddle his own canoe. There comes a time in every child's life when it must break forth into a world where he has to be on his own. Someone has observed that you help a moth out of its cocoon, and it is born weak and soon dies—let it break forth itself, and it enters the world vigorous and strong. Parents, if it is necessary for you to be reminded that a child must rely on itself, if it's the only way, you should be pricked as indicated. Dear parents, you yourself will determine "*what the harvest shall be.*"

STORY FORTY-EIGHT

"FILLET OF SOUL"

Not a "fillet of sole," but a "fillet of soul!" A "fillet of sole" is a fish with its backbone taken out. "A fillet of soul" is a man without any backbone. The world has never called so loudly for men who will stand on their own feet and do their thinking. Men who will stand by their convictions against odds are at a premium. There is a tendency for men, instead of weighing a thing on the basis of its being right or wrong, to determine which way the "wind is blowing" and set their sails accordingly. They are more ambitious to go along with popular sentiment than set their jaw for what is right and fair. Men are more prone to go with the crowd than to dare to be brave enough, "sink or swim, survive or perish," to stand by their convictions. Before they make a stand, they are too concerned with the popularity of the course they choose. "What is there in it if I vote this way? What prestige will it give me to go the other way?" Sometimes we care more about gaining favor than we do about championing the right.

I shall never forget as a child an Indian woman's coming to our back door begging flour. This clever Lamanite was a typical politician. My mother was always happy to learn that a newcomer to our home, Indian or otherwise, was a member of the Church. Our redskin beggar "sized" my mother right, and she voted accordingly. My mother's first question to our visitor was, "Are you a Mormon?" Now, note the cleverness of our Indian—before answering the question propounded she had a question to ask the head of the commissary. She asked my mother, "Are you a Mormon?" Mother answered in the affirmative. Then came the answer of our Indian friend: "So am I." And she got her flour. Yes, and if she were as good a politician at other doors at which she called as she was at ours, she had her provision sack full by nightfall.

Before I make a stand, before you make a decision, do we think only of the flour resultant and our popularity, or do we "do or die," after proper aim, dare pull the trigger?

The spots in history we are ashamed of are those scenes where actors on the stage lacked rigid vertebrae. Real history has been made by men who were not "fillets of soul." Our Church is meeting its destiny because we have had men and women of backbone. He who knows the weak are oppressed is a coward not to champion their cause. President Van

Buren, after listening to representatives of the Mormons, knowing full well the depredations against a God-fearing people, showed himself a "fillet of soul" when he dismissed that delegation with, "Your cause is just, but I can do nothing for you." Those weak words will ring throughout history as coming from a man without backbone.

Benedict Arnold was spineless. His courage could not stand the society and the bright lights of his Tory friends. His backbone turned to jelly, and he sold his country for money and influence. Yes, he showed some courage at Saratoga but later betrayed his country. After his betrayal he was given a commission in the English army, in the Carolinas. One day a captured American soldier was brought to him. The boy must have been Irish. When asked by Arnold what the colonists would do with him if they caught him (Arnold), his reply was: "If they caught you, they'd cut off that leg wounded in the Saratoga battle and give it a soldier's burial. Then they'd take the rest of your anatomy and hang it to the first apple tree they could find."

When John Hancock was given the privilege of signing the Declaration of Independence, in big letters he scrolled his name with this remark: "I will sign it large enough so that the king can read it without putting on his glasses." That took courage. John Hancock was not a "fillet of soul."

Patrick Henry, when he uttered in Virginia those famous words that rang around the world, "Give me liberty or give me death," showed fortitude that put the flame of patriotism in the soul of every American.

It was not "fillet of soul" in Martin Luther, when he denounced the sale of indulgences and burned in public his excommunication papers from the Catholic Church. It was backbone when he told his friends he would go to Worms if there were as many devils opposing him as tiles in the street. Because he dared stand out alone, following his conscience, he helped bring to us a new world.

Regulus, the Roman general imprisoned in Carthage, was given a furlough to go back to Rome and greet his family. He was promised his freedom if he would intercede with his country for an early peace with Carthage. He went back home and asked to be heard in the councils of war. Instead of following the instructions of his captors, to plead for peace, he told Rome that a strenuous attack by their army would defeat the Carthaginians. He kissed his wife and children and returned to Carthage to meet the death awaiting him. That took courage and a rigid vertebrae. Men like Regulus will never die. They are the men who illuminate history.

Only the backbone of a Lincoln dared tell his countrymen what was the real trouble in America. Only a man with a healthy spine would face a probable defeat that awaited such a diagnosis as, "A house divided against itself cannot stand."

It took men with spinal cords to win the war, men who were not "fillets of soul," who hoisted the stars and stripes against a rain of bullets, bombs, and strafing. The same courage that gave us liberty through Lexington and Concord, won the battles on the sea where such men as John Paul Jones showed no curvature of the spine. John Paul Jones is an inspiration: His ship was on fire; half of his men were dead or wounded. When the English captain ordered him to surrender Jones defiantly countered with, "We have just begun to fight."

Let's pause once in a while to take our hats off in reverence and appreciation to the leaders of our Church. May we never forget what we owe to the stamina of our Prophet Joseph Smith. May we always hold dear the undaunted fortitude and vision of Brigham Young in bringing twenty thousand people away from the garden of America to sagebrush and cacti. It was only a strong back with inspiration from the heavens that could plan and direct such a course.

One of the most popular games in America, even including golf and baseball is the game of "apple polishing." When your judgment is asked, give the "reason for the hope within you." Don't have your answer necessarily comply with what your asker would like your answer to be. If your boss asks you what you think of a certain proposition, tell him what you think, not what you think will "tickle his ears."

To be strong men we must make brave decisions. We cannot straddle the fence. I repeat again, some men take pride in not committing themselves. The question before them is not what is right, not what their conscience and judgment say is the right thing to do, but how may they act so that they gain favor. The world will always love the fellow with courage. He may lose the first round of the fight, but in the long run he will make history and be loved by those who love a strong man.

Millions ride on rubber tires, but let's not forget that only the courage of a Goodyear gave vulcanized rubber to us.

The boy who follows the plough would not be reading the Bible if a Tyndale hadn't been willing to face burning at the stake.

They tapped their heads when Columbus passed on the street, but only the spinal column of a Columbus could give us the New World.

The history of the world was changed because a Joseph, sold into Egypt, had the moral fiber to face his tempter and glorify the standards of his parents.

In politics, in Church, in our business, let's think things through carefully, but let it be said of us that we have backbone. Let us pray continually for proper guidance; let us seek the advice of those over us; let's not be "wishywashy." Let's not be like weather vanes, always pointing in the direction of the wind. Let us face the storms; let us stand on our feet. Let it not be said of us we are a "*fillet of soul.*"

STORY FORTY-NINE

LET'S SPRINKLE HER

They've left it too late. These fellows were determined to baptize this mother and her brood. They got along splendidly with the kittens, but it was a different story when they tried to immerse the old mother.

Let me tell you the story. I wish I knew where the story originated so I could give proper credit.

The lesson that particular morning in Sunday School had been "Baptism by Immersion." The teacher impressed the fact upon the class that the candidate was not to be sprinkled nor poured upon, but he was to go down under the water—to be completely covered; one only sprinkled would not land in too promising a place in the eternal regions.

Well, it wasn't surprising as the boys strolled into their yard to see this cat and her kittens by the side of the shed. These fellows were prompted to put into practice what they had learned in Sunday School. Aren't we taught, when we have learned a good lesson, to put it into operation as soon as we can? These lads were just as practical as they could be.

One got the tub; one ran for water; while the third corralled the feline family. The tub was soon filled and in less time than it takes to tell it each kitten in turn, under a strong and determined arm, went down and came up—not a dry hair on any one of them. Indeed it was a very complete operation—just as orthodox as the scriptures themselves intended.

But baptizing the cat was a different story entirely. She rebelled—she kicked—she scratched—and she drew the blood. She was not going to the realms above if that was the formula. After a five-round tussle and even a three to one break, her resistance was victorious. The boys were licked. In exasperation the lad receiving the most scratches vehemently cried out, "Oh, fellows, let's sprinkle her and let her go to the "Hot Place."

If those boys had had real interest in that mother cat's eternal welfare, they should have thought of her baptism many moons before.

"Train up a child in the way it should go: and when he is old, he will not depart from it."

Don't take the above story on baptism too seriously or I've made a mistake in telling it. There is more to the grand scheme of things than plenty of water and being completely immersed, but there's a great lesson here. Point the nose of the girl or the boy in the right direction before his bones are set too rigidly. Teach him righteousness . . . while his bones, if you please, are in the gristle stage.

Sometimes you will hear an unwise parent boast that he would not persuade his child to go to church until he is mature and able to think for himself. I am thinking of that wonderful hymn "Teach Me to Pray." Take a simple prayer away from a darling child, and you take something out of its life. I emphatically say you have robbed that child of the very dearest thing in the world.

A FATHER'S PRAYER

Dear God, my little boy of three
Has said his nightly prayer to Thee;
Before his eyes were closed in sleep
He asked that Thou his soul would keep.
And I, still kneeling at his bed,
My hand upon his tousled head,
Do ask, with deep humility
That Thou, dear Lord, remember me.

Make me kind, Lord, a worthy dad,
That I may lead this lad
In pathways ever fair and bright,
That I may keep his steps aright.
O, God, his trust must never be
Destroyed or even marred by me.

So, for the simple things he prayed
With childish voice so unafraid,
I, trembling, ask the same from Thee.
Dear Lord, kind Lord, remember me.
(From Chicago *Daily Tribune*—WGE Jr.)

Much has been said about plastic clay—human clay:

I molded with my power and art
A young child's warm and yielding heart.
The form I gave him still he bore,
But I could change him nevermore.
—Thomas Curtis Clark

You know one of the most wonderful things we work with these days is Portland cement, the cement we mix with sand, gravel, and water. It builds our houses, makes our roads, and makes our reservoirs. Before it sets you can do anything you want with it. If a leaf falls on a newly laid walk while it is "green," the imprint of that leaf will show every vein of the structure of the leaf for a hundred years after. Let an innocent dog chance to place his soft toes on that walk unnoticed by the workman, and that animal has left his "footprints on the sands of time" through the ages.

Mold the child's life while you can, before it is "set."

Have you observed these big trucks on the street conveying mixed concrete to the buildings under construction? It is an interesting contrivance—just like you'd mix a cake in the kitchen. They measure the sand, the gravel, and the water and then send it on its way to the job. All the time the load is traveling the bunker holding the mixture keeps turning, turning, turning. When it arrives it is just right—the huge "mix master" has just done its work well. As you saw that truck going along, did you ever wonder what would happen if something happened so that cement couldn't be dumped?

Sometime ago I heard a fellow in charge of a bunch of these machines, in the construction of Boulder Dam, tell what happened when one of them got stalled — the cement set right in the truck. In one hour the mass was plastic clay—in another hour it was solid granite. It cost a thousand dollars or more to chisel that concrete loose with sledge hammers.

That boy or girl of yours is like plastic concrete. Hold him while you can. Don't leave him until he "sets." If you want to see some examples of concrete set so that it has to be chiseled and blasted, go to one of our prisons. I repeat, those boys in Alcatraz Federal Prison cost you and me $7.00 a day or in thirty years it costs us the simple sum of $76,000.00 per boy.

Dear father and mother, the guardian angels, if you please, of those precious souls, don't let it be said of you "They left it too late."

STORY FIFTY

A THREE-ACT FARCE

Place—United States of America.
Time—1946.

Characters—fathers and mothers, their children, and politicians.

Act I. These old folks have been industrious and frugal. They have paid for the farm, and, as they dip into the winter of life, they find themselves with a few thousands in savings. Now comes the old age pension. These folks over sixty-five, if they can show technically that they haven't sufficient assets, may apply for the old age pension. With the help and inspiration from their offspring they have devised a way to get rid of their savings for old age and a rainy day and are passing this money over to their children. A very "wise" move—they are keeping their assets in the family circle and yet holding their hands out for monthly pensions from the government. Behind the scenes to promote this program stands the politician who beckons the old folks on with the subtle suggestion, "Come and get it. If you don't, someone else will."

Act II. Like Ananias and Sapphira of old who lied to Peter, these folks have cleared the deck and are now getting their allowance from the pension window.

Act III. Now we see the main characters of this sequence living on public funds and adjusting their consciences accordingly. In a large sense this is not a farce, but the most serious tragedy in the world. What kind of Being do they think rules the universe? Is he the Creator with an all-seeing eye whom you and I worship? Is he a Being that smiles on dishonesty and then accepts outward devotion and awards only pretense? "Consistency, thou art a jewel," or to put wholesome indignation in the language of Bobbie Burns:

> The man of independent mind,
> He looks and laughs at a' that.

Let me say here before going further: Show me how a generation treats its aged, and I'll show you the type of its civilzation. I should like it honestly said of me that I have always revered old age. I have tried to teach my children to honor the aged. Further, I glory in the fact that our government, state, and country cooperate to meet the emergency of taking care of the worthy incapacitated, whether it is from age or other infirmities. And with pride I rejoice that my Church has always played a leading role with a program that beckons to the unfortunate with food, raiment, and the needs of the body. Let us be clearly understood here. We are flaying only those who are parties to downright fraud and dishonesty.

Someone has said, and I repeat again, "Let's face the facts, if they kill us." Dear reader, don't think the above picture is overdrawn and don't dare to think all those who have joined the Ananias and Sapphira Club are those who don't know any better. I blush when I admit this, but if we are to believe half of what our welfare workers and bankers, and those who are in a position to know, are talking about, the above indictment is sad but true.

A banker in high standing in the community told us just a short time ago of an old gentleman who pretended to be religious and who proceeded to transfer from his savings account over five thousand dollars to his children so that he could receive forty dollars a month from the old age department. Another banker of equal repute told me this story: A man who made at least two thousand dollars that particular year collected monthly from the county forty dollars each for his wife and himself. Another gentleman of repute only a month or two ago gave an account to me of an old couple who came to him for advice asking how they could sell their property in such a way that the records would not show their holding title barring them from eligibility for old age benefits.

Yes, we can go on and on facing examples of dishonesty among our neighbors. If we are at all sensitive, our faces turn crimson in the realization of what some of our citizens are doing while pretending to believe in the fundamentals of the Ten Commandments. If these crimes were committed by the really aged whose steps had begun to totter with feebleness, we could make some allowances, but I'm sorry to admit that these dishonest roles are often played by those over sixty-five and in the very pink, you'd think, of judgment and right thinking. Yes, and what makes it worse in many cases, they are urged on by their sons and daughters who would rather get something for nothing dishonestly than earn their bread by honest endeavor.

Some of our western states have the highest population records in this whole United States of America of those over sixty-five getting government aid. Think of over forty out of every one hundred over this age being on government relief. We who are supposed to have influence with our fathers and mothers, just what are we thinking about? Our boys are now returning from charging up the ramparts, giving their lives for freedom, and we at home in a wholesome way in our attitude are fairly gnawing at the pillars sustaining liberty and justice. While thousands with the fervor that should prompt all of us to sacrifice for liberty, are giving, as it were, a good pail of milk, thousands are kicking the white liquid over.

Too many at home are scratching their heads scheming how they can, in the shrewdest way, tear the wing feathers from the American eagle. I repeat, America is going to turn one of the most spectacular somersaults ever recorded in the history of nations if we don't tumble to the seriousness of this bleeding that is going on. To say we are in the process right now in a gigantic way of killing the hen that lays the golden egg expresses it in language as weak as skimmed milk.

Some of us pretend to be really religious. Now you folks, whether the sons and daughters or parents, parties to these selfish manipulations, how can you reconcile your conduct with the lives of your pioneer or pilgrim forebears whom you pretend to honor for their sacrifices, with this double-crossing act that is being played on the stage of this wonderful land?

Let's have before us eternally, acting as a magnetic pole to our compasses of life, this simple word "honesty." Like a mariner going through the tempest of life, let it be our North Star. We can't go very wrong if we keep our bearings accordingly.

At our old home we always kept a cow. I remember Father always used to buy hay by the wagonload. He went to the market, chose his particular load, and in a few hours it was stuffed into the hayloft. It was always sold by official weight. If a farmer were unscrupulous enough to add a lot of water, sprinkled in the center of the load where it would not be easily detected, he might get away with it. (Of course, nobody in those days liked to pay ten dollars a ton for just plain water.) A farmer, of the type we are talking about, in the course of getting ready for marketing his hay one early morning, was heard to call out to his son in the yard, "John, put a dozen more buckets of water on the hay and hurry in to prayers."

Now that poor fellow was just thinking "bowlegged." His religion had a terrible case of malnutrition.

It doesn't make any difference what your religion is, when you kneel in prayer to give your thanks and offer your supplications, you want to do it with "clean hands."

Maybe I can make myself a little clearer by telling a story I heard one of my associates tell a year or so ago. It seemed that a man lived near the railroad tracks and used to get his winter's coal by going along the tracks with his wagon and picking up little pieces of coal, which had been knocked off the coal cars in the course of switching. Now it helped the man materially, and nobody objected.

But our friend wasn't willing to let well enough alone. One early morning while it was yet dark he was down near the coalyard, and the old Nick really tempted him. Satan found him entirely off guard. (I really think sometimes we blame the devil too much for our weaknesses.) Here's what happened:

The subject of our story had his team, and the wagon they were pulling was empty. Nobody seemed to be around on such a dark and frosty morning. He spied the chute whence the coal avalanched into the wagons by releasing the lever. It was just too much temptation. In a jiffy the team had been wheeled around, and the wagon was right in the path of the coal supply. In less time than it takes to tell it, he pulled the lever, and the coal flooded the wagon box. It came down that chute so fast and furious that the load broke the axle of the old fellow's wagon. Yes, he was stuck and with no way to unload. Out of the darkness appeared, as if by magic, the night watchman with his police badge fluttering in tune with his lantern. The officer had nothing else to do than his duty even if one of his friends was caught hands down. "John," said he, "I've just called the police station, but they may not get down here for half an hour. Let's go over to the depot. It's nice and warm over there, and we can have a warm cup of coffee while we're waiting."

John's eyes flashed, he raised up in his boots and looked defiantly into the face of the administrator of the law. His indignation broke loose, "I want you to know that drinking coffee is against my religion."

Again: "Oh, consistency, thou art a jewel."

What I am trying to say is, if you pretend to be devout you can't ride some items of your religion to death and leave honesty out of the picture. No man is really religious who isn't honest.

They tell a story of a negro's coming face to face with a strange inscription on a tombstone. It read, "I am not dead but sleeping." Looking down philosophically on that sacred spot the old fellow observed, talking aloud to his friend under six feet of ground, "Well, pal, you're just fooling yourself, that's all."

Now you folks that are in this skin game we are talking about, with one hand fleecing the government and with the other petitioning for a ringside reservation in the realms above, if I read the scriptures right, "Well, pal, you're just fooling yourself, that's all."

I am talking to you sons and daughters of these folks under fire as well as to the old folks themselves. Do you ever imagine your grandfathers and grandmothers or your great-grandparents looking down on you from above as you stoop to this dishonesty? They gave their "all" for their country and some for their religion. No sacrifice was too great either for their country or their religious convictions. What do you suppose they think of you, their flesh and blood!

STORY FIFTY-ONE

BISHOP, IS A CLIQUE RUNNING YOUR WARD?

Bishop, if your ward is run by a clique sitting in the back, you are going to fail just as surely as this fellow in the picture is going to run into that steel post. A clique can mean many things. We have heard of its being a bishop's wife— with or without her friends. Some such housewife was once heard to say something like this "Yes, my husband presides in our home, but you bet your life I conduct the exercises." Sometimes it can be a club or group of people who meet formally or informally once or twice a month; Yes, sometimes you find a family and their friends commander and chief of the ward's policies and destinies.

Bishop, with the help of your Heavenly Father and your good counselors, with your ear to the councils of the priesthood, reign with dignity unfettered. If some people in your ward had their way they'd handle you like some political bosses prescribe the heart beat of those they engineer into office. But, bishop, thank the heavens you were not given your office that way. You were placed there after prayer by those having proper authority, and then you were sustained by the people. And, remember, if you will listen to the voice of the people, that voice coming through the channels as prescribed by the Church, you can't go wrong. There is safety in the counsel of many. Give ear to the most humble child.

As a child I remember most vividly a billboard ad of a big packing company. It was a time when they were pushing beef extract very hard on the market. That was a clever picture. It showed a whole herd of corn fed steers crushed into the mill to make this famous soup. You saw the prize cattle going into one end and the can of soup being drawn out the other. If I remember correctly, the ad read, "A Herd in Every Can."

I repeat, advice to a bishop should not come from one source. It should come from the whole herd—then your soup will contain all the vitamins.

How does the bee get his supply of honey? He gets it by going from flower to flower. And the beautiful part of it is that the flower gives and takes, and the exchange of courtesies, so to speak, benefits both the bee and the flower. The bee gets its food from the flower, and the flower is benefited by the bee in that the bee scatters the pollen from flower to flower. Yes, bishop, and don't forget the same thing is true with you and your people. As you seek advice from them, your administration, if I may use that term, is magnified, and you dignify and encourage the growth of your people.

Bishop, don't be run by a clique. The gospel plan has given you two counselors. Meet with them regularly and often—lean on them and let them lean on you. Let prayer and humility and a chin set for standing by the right guide your destiny, and you will never go wrong.

STORY FIFTY-TWO

BISHOP, ARE YOU STANDING IN THE WAY OF PROGRESS?

Are you as it were an old model, and are others, anxious to get along on the road, held back? In using the word *model* we mean *attitude*. Are you driving in this generation with an attitude of two generations ago? Are you driving a broken-down horse with a dilapidated harness and wagon, and is an eight-cylinder streamline motor trying to pass you? Are you holding up the whole procession?

Sometime ago in a Church group, in talking Church statistics, someone was led to observe that there was, during the year, quite a turnover of bishops. Someone in the meeting who had recently had some experience with a bishop or two whom he thought not up on their toes, was heard to comment, "*and some of them won't turn over.*" Now, that's quite an accusation, but if the cap fits any of us let's have this observation spur us up rather than resent it.

In most of our up-to-date paint stores, they have what they call an agitator. If a can of paint stands without being stirred, the lead sinks to the bottom and before it can be used you have to tip the can upside down, put it in the agitator, and with the aid of an electric current shake the daylights out of the contents.

We wonder sometime if we as individuals, when we get dead on our feet and stale, shouldn't be put through some kind of agitator and put in motion. To repeat, sometimes don't we get *metallurgic fever?* Some wide-awake M. D. diagnosed the case as follows: "Metallurgic fever is that disease caused by the iron in the blood turning to lead and sinking to the seat of the trousers." In other words, it is a terrible state of inertia where indications point to coagulation of the blood and semi-coma.

Bishop, let's not stand in the way of progress. Let's not have a whole string of cars honking behind us with us taking up the road, stopping the procession. Let's be up and doing, —getting things done,—leading the procession. "If anything is going on, be thou in it."

STORY FIFTY-THREE

BISHOP, ARE YOU IN A RUT?

Someone has wisely observed, "The only difference between a rut and a groove is that one is deeper than the other."

Bishop, do you remember those old wagon ruts we used to get into in the days before the auto and the paved road? It was terrible when you once got in them, and it was dangerous. Often an axle or wagon tongue was broken in trying to get out of the way of an oncoming vehicle. The moral of the story is, don't travel in ruts. When once people got in them, between hook and crook, they did get out, but the operation was hazardous as well as painful. But we're talking about roads—yes, bishop, we're talking about you and your job, too. Are you in a rut? If you are, get out quick, and when you get out, stay out.

It is said of a fellow somewhat sluggish of mind and rather behind the times that, "His mind was so slow that his remarks were invariably late, arriving just in time to see the topic of the moment steaming out of the station."

A certain professor not noted too much for progress was described as "a dismal soul who embalmed the subject and let us view the remains."

Bishops, we have too much respect for you splendid God-fearing men to insinuate, but all of us in regards to keeping up with the times never were on the spot as we are these days. The world is moving fast, and, in a sense, we've got to go with it. Without this attitude and help from the heavens, we are hopeless and helpless. But let's be abreast of the times and be alert to the changing conditions about us.

Yes, Brigham Young used oxen, and his de luxe conveyance was a white top or buckboard, but he used the latest models he could find. If he were living today, the possibilities are he'd use a twelve-cylinder car and an express airline. Those men were on their toes and alert and were the type of material the Lord undoubtedly likes to work with.

Bishop, young folks won't be too demonstrative in their feelings to you, but particularly these days they are praying that you as their bishop will be alive to their problems. Keep out of the ruts. Never mind how they did things fifty years ago. How should they be done today?

STORY FIFTY-FOUR

Don't Be A Lobster

The way the story goes, a Hawaiian was out fishing for lobster. He had caught a couple and had placed them in some sort of pan. The sidewalls on the lip of the pan were not very high. A stranger came up and remarked to the fisherman,

"Why didn't you get a deeper pan or bucket in which to place those lobsters? When your back is turned, they will crawl out." Then came the answer from the fisherman: "Friend, you just don't know lobsters. One lobster will never let the other get up higher than himself if he can help it. If one of those lobsters makes a move to get out or higher in the world, his fellow prisoner will always jerk him back."

When I heard that story, I thought what a lesson there was in it. Do we as brothers, as friends, or what not, through envy or jealousy, hold one another back? If one of us gets a little higher in the world than the other, do we instinctively want to pull him down or stop his progress? You know, jealousy is one of the worst things in the world. It does hurt us sometimes to see others progress.

They were having a school program. Every mother was there, each one proud or envious depending upon the importance of the roles her children were playing. A pompous little fellow came to the platform and with all the oratory of Patrick Henry shouted to the skies: "Friends, Romans, countrymen, lend me your ears." This display of eloquence was too much for an envious mother. She turned to her seat-mate and with her nose pointed upward proclaimed: "That's the Jones kid. He wouldn't be his mother's son if he wasn't trying to borrow something."

Two street sweepers were sitting on the street curb soliloquizing together. One of their profession had just passed to the Great Beyond. Speaking of their deceased friend, one street employee observed to the other, "Bill was a great street sweeper." "But," observed his companion sitting beside him, "didn't you think he was a little weak around the lamp posts?"

"Now when Jesus was born in Bethlehem of Judaea in the

days of Herod the king, behold, there came wise men from the east to Jerusalem,

"Saying, Where is he that is born King of Jews? for we have seen his star in the east, and are come to worship him.

"When Herod the king had heard these things, he was troubled, and all Jerusalem with him." (Matt. 2:1-3.)

The king was troubled because he wanted no competition in his holding the scepter. The people with good cause were troubled because they know well to what ends a Herod would go to remove this obstacle.

And this is only one black chapter in the thousands of stories of bloodshed in history—the result of jealousy and envy. Thousands of innocent babies were butchered in the streets like cattle because of the selfishness of one soul.

I ask you, dear reader, are you free from this venom that has curdled the blood of the inhabitants of the world since history began? Are you pleased to rejoice at the accomplishments of your friends, or are you envious? When you hear of a relative or friend going places in the world, is there gladness in your soul or does the reptile of envy entwine around your throat, choke the virtue within you, asserting itself? Putting it frankly, are you made happy or are you full of hate because another is up a little higher on the ladder than you?

Don't be a lobster. If your companion can get a little higher than you, don't pull him back.

> Oh, jealousy,
> Thou ugliest fiend of hell! Thy deadly venom
> Preys on my vitals, turns the healthful hue
> Of my fresh cheek to haggard sallowness,
> And drinks my spirit up.
>
> —Hannah Moore

Nothing written tells plainer what jealousy will do than the story of Shakespeare's *Othello*.

You see to what length this poison will go, and to what depths a villain will go when this poison we are talking about gets him under its power. Yes, and to go a little further, how the whitest rose will be crushed in the calloused hands of jealousy. I am talking about beautiful Desdemona, the traitor Iago, and the champion of honor, the brave Moorish general, Othello. Iago was jealous of his fellow officer Cassio because the latter had been advanced to a position Iago wanted himself. He set a trap for the good Cassio and lowered him to the dust. Then he plotted against his commander, accusing Desdemona of infidelity until in a rage of jealousy the Moor himself killed his lovely wife and then took his dagger out and put an end to his own life. As the boy would say, this was a double feature in this story of jealousy.

Pick up the history of any nation. There is a trail of murder and crime as a result of this thing called jealousy. Brothers poisoning brothers to get the throne is an act played throughout the ages.

Jealousy is a cancer of the worst type, and like a cancer, the only hope of escaping its terrible punishment is to destroy it in its very early stages—when it's in miniature. It is better by far not to let it get the slightest encouragement to fasten itself to your anatomy. Jealousy is like the octopus of the seas.

Another person we read of in holy writ, in a fit of jealousy, slew his brother. Ever since this chapter when Cain played this role with his brother, this octopus of the human make-up has been taking its toll.

When your brother, your friend, and even your competitor, attains recognition in this or that, rejoice with him if you can. Then you show your bigness—then you show you are proud to be called one of God's children.

Are you a musician? Do you get envious of the other fellow when he sings or plays well? Are you a mechanic?

Do you rejoice when another is skillful? Are you ambitious as a speaker? Do you feel bad if a competitor, as it were, in this business of oratory does very well? Are you an artist? Is there resentment in your soul when another artist gains recognition for a portrait or a landscape? To put it frankly and clearly, if one of your fellows strides ahead even to pass you, just how big are you? Are you a pigmy or giant in your soul?

Don't be a lobster.

While attending a stake conference a few months ago I heard President George F. Richards tell a story that warmed me to the bones. It was a story of Cain and Abel *in reverse*. Here's the story:

Abram and Zimri had worked harmoniously together for years. Their main crop was wheat. One night during harvest time they had spent considerable time in confiding together, as brothers will. The result of this meeting was that each brother went to his home with some rather definite plans for the night. Something happened in the exchange of confidence that brought the hearts of these two souls even a little closer than ever. Each went to his bed with some definite resolutions.

Abram arose from his bed. Said he to himself, "When I go home at night a loving wife greets me with a well-cooked supper, and my children climb upon my knee. Zimri goes home to a cold house with no one to put a kiss upon his brow. I'll arise and take some of my sheaves and place them upon his heap." He arose and with the help of the moon increased the heap of his brother's grain.

But Zimri, too, was stirred with an emotion that had to be satisfied with a like noble deed. Thought he, "As Abram goes to his home tonight, there are many more mouths to feed than there are under my roof. Unknown to him I will take some of my sheaves and place them upon his heap." He arose from his bed and carried sheaves to increase his brother's heap. Then he went to bed to pleasant dreams.

Lo and behold, the next morning as each one visited his piles of grain, he noticed that it looked about the same although some sacrifice had been made in each case in the direction of the other's heap.

The next night Abram took his sheaves again and carried them to the grain of his brother and then lay behind his own heap to solve the mystery. He didn't have to wait long. His brother, with the same emotions, was increasing the granary of Abram.

Abram arose and caught his brother Zimri in his arms and wept upon his neck and kissed his cheek, and Zimri saw the whole and could not speak, neither could Abram for their hearts were full.

. . . . . Sweeter sings the brooklet by,
Brighter beams the azure sky,
Oh, there's One who smiles on high,
When there's love at home.

STORY FIFTY-FIVE

BISHOP, DO YOU PLAN YOUR WORK?

Bishop, would you start to build a house before you had a blueprint? You wouldn't start even a little shed before you had pretty well in mind its dimensions, roof structure, but in your responsibilities as bishop when you come before your people, do they feel from the time you open your month that you with your counselors have planned the proposition well? Have you thought it through? Do you see the end from the beginning? Have you, figuratively speaking, well in mind how each part in the plan fits with the other part?

Nothing will put the members of your ward to sleep more quickly than when you lack definiteness, and they can see you have come to the meeting unprepared. If you are not prepared, your group will be watching the clock, dozing, and look as if they didn't care whether school kept or not. In the cartoon it's different, they are attentive because they are listening to a leader who knows where he is going. You show us a bishop who, in a prayerful way, plans his work and has those at his right hand and left hand help him plan, and we'll show you a ward that does things and is going places. A leader who plans his work inspires his followers. George Washington was a great leader. He was a greater planner than he was a genius. The first president of the United States didn't make a move until he had thought it through, even his retreats. Napoleon said of Washington's retreats that they were among the greatest victories in military history. Anthony Wayne, one of his greatest generals, was once heard to say, "I will attack hell itself if George Washington will plan it." Yes, bishop, your people will go to the very ends of the earth and, yes, to the bottom of their pocketbooks if what you want is well-planned.

A boy in giving a narration, when coming to the exciting part of the story, exclaimed, "The hero arrived on the scene, jumped on his horse, dug in the spurs, and charged in all directions."

Bishop, do you ride in all directions, or do you methodically follow up step by step a well-defined plan? Your constituents want leadership; they don't want noise. They want light and guidance and not fits of thunder. They tell a story of an old Negro, who while returning to his home with his mule and cart, was caught in a terrible rainstorm. It came down in such bucketfuls that he couldn't see a rod in front of him. It got so bad, he was so bewildered and so much in the dark that he didn't know where he was going. Rain or no rain, he had to get out and lead the mule by the bit. All the time the thunder was terrific. It seemed the earth would shake to pieces and gobble him up or throw him over the precipice. The bolts from the heavens pretty nearly scared him to death. His only hope in this catastrophe was that once in a big while there would be a flash of lightning—for a split second, he could see his way ahead a few feet and move with safety. If he only had more lightning! It got so bad that he would wait for a flash of lightning, move a few feet ahead, and then wait a few minutes for another flash. He was a nervous wreck; he could stand that thundering no longer. He fell on his knees, stretched his arms to heaven, and shouted in desperation, "Oh, Lord, if it is just the same to you, let's have a little more light and not quite so much noise."

Bishop, plan your work. Nothing will inspire your people more than plans and specifications of what you have ahead.

BISHOP, DO YOU PITY YOURSELF?

Bishop, when you look into the mirror is this what you see? There are many persons who have suggested with good grace an Eleventh Commandment. Here is one with considerable merit: "Thou shalt not pity thyself, for in the day thou pitiest thyself, thou art on a dead center."

Pity when given to others may be a virtue, but is a most deadly drug when administered to yourself.

Bishop, in plain American English, to use a quotation often used by President J. Reuben Clark, Jr., Rule No. 6, "Don't take yourself so seriously."

Henry Ford says, "Nothing is particularly hard if you divide it into small jobs." Take the same time you spend in pitying yourself in removing those burdens from your back to the backs of others, and let these good officers have the thrill of being responsible to you and your counselors. Bishop, are you a pack horse or are you a leader? If you are inclined to place too many burdens on yourself, count ten, "Stop, Look, and Listen," and remove those bundles one at a time onto others. May we repeat here, "It is better to keep ten men working than doing ten men's work." Learn to shed your worries. The sycamore is too rigid. The snow breaks its limbs to pieces. The pine takes all the snow it can and lets the rest slide off. Learn to shift your troubles but shift them to others.

Bishop, do you see your responsibilities clearly or do you "see through a glass darkly?" Occasionally get a few feet away from yourself so you can see yourself and your duties with proper vision. Figuratively speaking, are your glasses clean? If they're not, your road ahead will be blurred, and you won't move forward with accuracy and dispatch.

Sometime ago the question came up whether or not we should clean the statue of the Angel Moroni on the temple. This matter was brought definitely to us when a steeplejack was in town. We were doing some painting and cleaning of flagstaffs on our buildings, and other high jobs which the ordinary painter was not inclined to tackle. We had been given a price of eighty-five dollars for the cleaning of the statue. Several of us who had the responsibility of deciding this were looking steadfastly up toward the golden monument, inspected at two hundred fifty feet below, trying to decide whether or not we should have this particular work done. One of the group in observing the optical instruments that one of the Presiding Bishopric was peering through to make the decision observed, "Bishop, if you'll clean your glasses you'll save the Church eighty-five dollars." The glasses were cleaned, and the Church was saved eighty-five dollars.

Bishop, as you look at yourself, get a clear vision. Don't pity yourself, but divide up your work.

STORY FIFTY-SEVEN

DON'T FENCE ME IN

"Don't fence me in." Youth, that's what you say to your fathers and mothers. Youth, that's what you cry to your teachers in school. That's the language many of you use in your rebellion against some of us who would interfere with you and your rights as freeborn American youth.

With a twinkle in his humorous eyes, Brigham Young, one of the greatest friends to red-blooded Mormon lads and lassies, is reported to have said, "You young people *think* we old people are fools. We *know* you are."

Youth, let me get close enough to you to see the whites of your eyes and talk to you. One humorist observed something like this: When a kid reaches the ripe age of seventeen, he looks at his father and wonders how long it will be before his father will know as much as he knows. When he becomes twenty-five years of age, he marvels how fast his dad has progressed in the realm of learning and understanding.

This cartoon of our lamb was taken from a photo used by the *Arizona Highways*. When I spied it I told Jim Smith, one of the highway commissioners, that whether he liked it or not I was going to have Bywater, our cartoonist, make an ink copy of it and use it. He made no objection, and here it is.

Now this venturesome lamb—you can see by the set of his jaw and squint of his eyes that he'd like to break through that fence and do some exploring. You don't have to do any tall thinking to tell in a jiffy that there is something across this Mason and Dixon line that is mighty interesting. The only thing that is holding him back is that forked stick with a piece of baling wire held over his head. That stops his taking part in the game on the highway or in the field adjoining.

Now that half-grown sheep, although he is "dead sure" he could conquer the world with the flip of his little hoof, still needs its mother. When mealtime comes around, he will get up close to his mother and demand refreshments from the commissary department. When the night gets dark, and he hears the yelp of the coyote, he will cuddle up close to that warm fleece, the owner of which gave him birth. For weeks from the time he had learned the mechanics of getting his daily nourishment, he had been satisfied to stay close enough to her to hear her beck and call, but lately he has nibbled a few tendrils of grass and thinks he's grown up and craves other worlds to conquer.

Youth, you are just like that lamb. Yes, we fence you in. Yes, and then sometimes when you get too hilarious, we get a forked stick to keep you from breaking through. "Don't fence me in," you cry, and in plain English, just where would you land if you had your entire way? Some of you, in less time than it takes to tell it, would lose your hide and land in a lump on one of the highways of life.

Happy is the boy or girl who has confidence in his parents to the extent that he will sit up close to them and take their advice. Boys and girls, we have been in the forest for many years—we know the game trails. We know of those who lie in wait to fleece you. We know the wolves in that field next door who would take advantage of your innocence and skin you alive. There are reptiles in that dark forest who, if they got you off guard, would twine themselves around your anatomy python snake fashion and crush the life's blood out of you. That's why we want to fence you in. This little lamb has never met a coyote; he doesn't know the destruction of the slap of the paw of a grizzly or the terrible accuracy of the fangs of the timber wolf.

Yes, we are talking in parables, but we are not telling you fairy tales. We are talking real life. You don't like that forked stick nor the fact that we have fenced you in. We are only trying to save you against yourself.

I repeat, boys and girls, we want to protect you against yourselves. President David O. McKay has told a story of a beautiful colt on his ranch, one of those colts that they weren't very successful in fencing. He would go through the fences, untie the rope on the gate, and do everything but unlock the padlock. He would no sooner be in a field and thought secure than they would find him breaking over the traces. He was really a problem, but they loved him because of his beauty and strength. One day he broke through, got into a granary where there was a sack of grain poisoned for gophers. Their beautiful animal that day stretched out cold in death because he didn't see the wisdom of honoring the safeguards placed for his benefit.

"Eternal vigilance is the price of security."

A painting struck me very forcefully a few years ago. It was a picture of a mountain lion and her two cubs resting on the brink of a precipice such as you might see everywhere in the Grand Canyon of the Colorado. The mother of those kittens watched every move her children made. Overhead soared an eagle. What a dainty morsel for breakfast one of those young cats would make! Yet, no maneuver of that carnivorous bird escaped her vigilant eye. The mother knew too well that other enemies would take from her those she loved, or that one false move in the capers of those cubs would land them with every bone in their bodies splintered to bits, a thousand feet below the rock where they rested. I repeat, on that stage the lioness was playing a major role in "eternal vigilance." She knew that was the price of security for her brood.

Boys and girls, your parents are as anxious of your welfare as that big cat of the Rockies was for her cubs. If we watch every move you make, it is only because you are sitting, as it were, on a precipice where one false move would make you a "goner." There are wolves in the forest and eagles in the air, and if it weren't for the vigilance of those who love you, you'd be torn to pieces.

Youth, we've lived longer than you have—that's why we know better than you the "booby traps," the hidden mines that would blow you to atoms.

I said we were not talking fairy tales to you. We're not. Aesop wrote some fables that have value. At least once a year read Aesop's *Fables*. They will keep your mind and judgment physically fit.

Let me tell you one of those stories—it fits here. A lion once radioed throughout the neighborhood that he was sick nigh unto death and summoned all the animals to come to hear his last will and testament. (Curiosity will kill a cat, and others, too.) The first to enter the cave of the king of beasts was a lamb followed by a calf. The lion seemed to recover his health and strength immediately after the visit of those unsuspecting creatures. He came to the mouth of his cave, and there beheld a fox who had been waiting outside for some time. "Why don't you come in to pay your respects to me?" said the lion to the fox. "I beg your majesty's pardon," observed the wise little animal, "but I noticed the tracks of the animals that have already come to you, and while I see hoof marks going in, I see none coming out. Till the animals that have entered your cave come out, I prefer to remain outside."

Now if I use my imagination, before that lamb broke through the fence and galloped to the home of the lion, I can hear him mutter as he runs, "Don't fence me in." If that young lamb had stayed close to its mother, the lion wouldn't have had mutton for breakfast. If that young heifer hadn't jumped the traces that day and disregarded the old cow's advice, she wouldn't have had her name that day in the obituary columns of the town paper.

Young folks, there is always a juicy bait on a hidden hook waiting to land you when you are not on your guard. There is a predatory animal along every path of the forest crouching in the grass waiting to take advantage of your innocence. Young lady, there are innkeepers who are happy in the profit on a pint of whisky even though that profit means the losing of your virtue. Young man, there is an army of men that would stay up all night and spend a hundred dollars on you to get you to take your first drink and make another customer for John Barleycorn. Yes, there are a thousand vicious "joint" keepers in every American city of any size that spider-fashion would spin a web to catch a boy or girl off guard.

We older folks know this, and many of you young people don't know it, but we stand on the border of the forest like an old hunter to warn an innocent traveler of the man-eating tigers and lions lying in wait. Believe us, young folks, we stand as a lighthouse to warn you of the treacherous rocks just under the waves that would dash your little soul crafts to pieces. "Many brave souls are asleep in the deep, so beware, beware."

> Let the lower lights be burning;
> Send a gleam across the wave;
> Some poor fainting, struggling seaman
> You may rescue; you may save.

Now, folks, that's the only role we want to play. We have been tossed about on the stormy waves of life, and we know where the rocks are. After all, there is no substitute for experience. We have been exposed to the elements, and some of us are carrying around with us a little rheumatism as a result of exposure.

With his joints all double sized and crippled up, a wise old fellow down South was heard to advise, "What good is rheumatics if they can't tell you what the weather is going to be?"

You of the next generation, *we* know what the weather will be, and we don't want you to expose yourself too completely and get yourselves all wet. Young lady, your mother doesn't want you to be tied to her apron strings. Young man, we don't want you to be a hot-house plant or a "panty-waist." We want you to be vigorous, courageous entities, able to face the storms of life. When we were your age, we were just as human as you are now. We were no better than you are, but don't forget we who have weathered best are we who heeded the advice of our parents. It means just what it says, "Honour thy father and thy mother"—just why?—"That thy days may be long upon the earth."

We don't want to be regimental of every move you make. You don't like that program, and you shouldn't. All we want to do is, with our arms around you, guard you against the pitfalls of life.

Next time your soul rebels against our cautions to you, "Stop, look, and listen," think before you leap. You know, we could make a wonderful team, you with your vitality and vigor and we, with forty or more years' experience, walking side by side with you to help you appreciate the things that have made us happy. Yes, and we'll get around the piano and sing with you to our hearts content "*Don't Fence Me In.*"

STORY FIFTY-EIGHT

BISHOP, ARE YOU DOING IT THE EASY WAY?

Bishop, look at the faces of these ward members. They're happy to give if they know where you're going. They'll get on the "band wagon" with you if you will plan with them. The day of letting each organization tantalize promiscuously the members of your ward for money is ancient history. Your good people want only to know what the whole bill is, and they'll come through with the greatest pleasure in the world. Folks will pay many times as much in a lump sum as they will in little dabs that continually annoy them.

The officers of your ward will accomplish infinitely more if they don't have to be eternally worried with the responsibility of dunning the people of the ward for finances for their particular organization.

Bishop, do this job the easiest way. The hard way is the most inefficient and full of grief. Intelligent direction makes the burden light.

They tell a story of an Irish policeman that one morning in going about his beat found a dead horse on one of the streets in his district, namely Marlborough Street. Of course, he had to make a report of this unusual story. The trouble with Pat was that he didn't know how to spell "Marlborough." He asked first the sergeant how to spell the word. The sergeant only chuckled, and then our executive of the law asked the girl in the office. She had a twinkle in her eye, too. In fact, the office was delighted to see their Irish friend in such difficulty, but he wasn't happy at all in their being so elated at his expense. He grabbed his hat, and, as he went out, he nearly tore the door off its hinges. He was really mad.

The sergeant observing the demeanor of his friend officer called him: "Pat, what are you going to do?" Then came the answer. "I'm going out and move that d-- horse over on *Maple* Avenue."

Bishop, there is always a hard way to do things or an easy way. Mark Twain's story of Tom Sawyer and whitewashing the fence will go down in history as one of the finest examples of "doing it the easiest way." Tom did it the easy way. There was enthusiasm in the group, and everyone wanted to help, even if each had to "dig up."

STORY FIFTY-NINE

BISHOP, WHICH ONE ARE YOU?

"*Budgeting is the means of telling a dollar where to go instead of wondering where it went,*" or in other words, bishop, are you running the dollar or is the dollar running you? If it is running you, it will surely take you for a real ride. You won't know where you are or in what direction you are going.

There is a story of an old Negro out fishing in a boat. I guess he must have caught a decidedly much bigger fish than he expected. In fact it was so big, it was just dragging him and his boat around the lake. The darky was as concerned as he was surprised. In exasperation the old fellow nervously trying to decide whether to let go or hold on, yelled at the water monster. "What I would like to know is—am I *fishing* or are you *niggering?*"

Bishop, half of your ward problems will be solved if you will get on the budget plan with the rest of the bishops. Get into a huddle with your counselors. Select a good committee. Put it up to your people, and they will change what appears to be a burden into a delight.

STORY SIXTY

BISHOP, ARE YOU TRYING TO DO TOO MUCH?

Are you trying to cover too many eggs? If you are, some eggs are going to get cold and won't hatch. In fact, if this hen in the picture hatches any at all it will be a wonder.

A farmer had instructed his boy to set the hen. He reported to his father that the job had been completed.

"How many eggs did you put under her, Bill?"

"Forty, Dad."

"But, Son, she can't cover that many."

"I know it, Dad, but I like to see the darn fool spread herself."

Now, bishop, don't fool yourself. No matter how anxious you are to do many things, you can do just so much. You are like the hen; your coverage is limited. You can spread yourself just so far.

Now, bishop, the very nature of your responsibilities is such that you must have your interest in many things. One who would observe otherwise would be very poor of vision. However, if you are going to supervise well, you can't take care of too many details. You must delegate the hatching of many of the eggs to others.

Are you trying to make all of the decisions or are you so organized in your ward that others are making decisions that concern their particular assignments? Bishop, remember we are all human. We like to do a job well. A person is odd if he doesn't want a responsibility placed upon him. Whether it be great or small, he likes the *tingle,* if you please, of pleasing those over him. Bishop, the people of your ward want you to give them something to do and have the satisfaction of a pat on the back when it is done. Divide up your work. Many hands make light work. Bishop, glory in the achievements of others—your big job is to see others grow. You will be measured by the lieutenants you develop and not by the fuss you make in spreading yourself to cover all the eggs in the nest.

Bishop, in your job are you trying to be the mayor, the city commission, the dog catcher, and the garbage collector as well? Are you trying to be the whole show? Do you corral for yourself personally all the work? Leave a little for the other fellow. You'll live longer upon the land; you'll reign with more dignity and prestige if you will honor others with their share of the work to be done. Don't try to play the bass fiddle, the violin, the trombone, the saxaphone, and the bugle, thrown in. Let each man and woman in your domain, including those fine counselors you have chosen, play his particular instrument, and your administration will be marked with harmony and efficiency.

There is no substitute for experience. Put some of those eggs under others and hold them responsible, and by so doing you will increase your capacity and influence, and your members will be more happy and grow with you.

STORY SIXTY-ONE

BISHOP, DO YOU ANSWER YOUR MAIL?

Now this poor fellow looks as if he's taken a day off to open his mail, and so far he's only half through. He has left it so long that he's had to take a nap in the middle of the ordeal —and if his face tells the right story, he's surely in misery. He has let his mail so accumulate that it appears now as an insurmountable task ahead. Someone has said, "Putting off an easy thing makes it hard; putting off a hard thing makes it impossible."

Bishop, if we don't answer your mail, you are bewildered, and when you don't answer our mail, we are at a loss to know what to do. Sometimes important things are stymied because either you or we haven't been prompt in acknowledging letters that should receive an answer. Building programs are held up indefinitely sometimes because we've asked you a question, and we wait and wait for an answer. Much money is lost, very much inconvenience is caused because our office fails or you fail to drop a line and spend three cents.

We appreciate, and we hope you also make allowances, that there are times when it is impossible to write promptly, but even if you are going to be delayed in answering some questions fully or given complete information, drop a card so we will know what to do. If we're not mistaken, there's a hymn we often sing at funerals—sometimes it hums in our heads at the Presiding Bishop's Office when we walk the floor jumping up and down, as it were, because some good bishop will not answer our mail—the hymn, I think, is, "Unanswered Yet."

Now, bishop, to be fair with you, sometimes in this matter our office is at fault. When we are, a gentle reminder will be no offense. We'll forgive you if you'll forgive us. In this matter of answering letters let's all tighten our belts and resolve to be more prompt. Let our slogan be, "Do it now." Let's not let the spiders weave their webs over the box dedicated to unanswered mail. Let's have no *Dead Letter* office in our respective realms.

STORY SIXTY-TWO

BISHOP, ARE YOU CIVIC MINDED?

Bishop, do you make it your business to be interested in the affairs of your town? Is your work or business and your Church absorbing all of your time? Do you hold yourself immune from civic affairs? If you do, you are making a mistake. Nothing will help your influence among your people more than for them to know you are a "live wire" in things that concern us as citizens and members of society in general. Once in a while we find a fellow so absorbed in his Church duties that he's dead to all that's happening outside of his small natural world. In other words, he's *smug*. And when a fellow's smug, he's on dangerous ground. So many times we find some of our people complaining of evils in a community, but they themselves are doing nothing to correct these evils. The very nature of your position, bishop, is such that your word will go a long way in influencing those things a community should have. Do you set the right example to your people in being interested in better roads, better schools, and better bridges? Should the district you live in have a better water supply? All these matters for the sake of ultimate good to the Church and your people, you should interest yourself in. Maybe your town would be enjoying a better water system, and there would be less disease in your town and more comfort if you'd put your shoulder to the wheel.

Ours is a practical religion, and our leaders from Joseph Smith down have interested themselves in civic affairs. We had a pre-existent life; we have our lives here on mother earth; and we have a life to live over the horizon. If this is our philosophy, then this life is as important as any other. Let's make the most of it. Yes, let us team with our fellow citizens in anything that means the betterment of our conditions, that means happiness and progress.

Bishop, we are not advocating your joining every club in town and so dividing your valuable time and energy so that your family will never see the color of your eyes. A bishop can have his mind on so many things that he's like the cat turned loose on ten mice—she didn't catch any of them. But on the other hand, men should not crawl in a little hole and spin a web around themselves. To get in a rut of any kind is bad. Someone has wisely said, "Every man, no matter what his aims in life may be, business, professional, or what not, will make a better job in attaining that goal if he will emphasize the *spiritual*." But all attention given to what's over the horizon will make a man narrow-minded. Cement is one of the strongest things in the world, but straight cement mixed with nothing else will crack. The good job is done when cement is mixed with clean sand and reinforced with steel.

Bishop, let's have vision and viewpoint just as broad as we can. This is a big world, and we're all God's children.

In the shell the little bird's life was encompassed with only shell—the little creature thought the whole world was made of pale blue shell. One day he hatched out and thought the whole world was made of nothing but feathers and hair and sticks— this was the lining of his nest, and as yet he hadn't looked over its walls. But one day he got strong enough to climb to the top of the nest—now he saw nothing but the green leaves of the tree—he thought the whole world was green. One day he had the experience of being pushed out of the nest by his wise parents. Now he saw not a world of just pale blue shell, of only nest lining, of only just green leaves, but a world of mountains, plains, oceans, and vastnesses everywhere.

Bishop, if there is anything lovely or of good report, let's seek after these things.

STORY SIXTY-THREE

BISHOP, ARE YOU WATCHING FIRE HAZARDS?

This blaze could happen to your Church. Seventy-four years ago a cow in Chicago "kicked the bucket." We don't mean that she died—she just kicked the bucket. The bucket hit a lantern or candle and that was the cause of Chicago's burning down.

One year's fire losses in the United States were estimated at $403,000,000.00. While, of course, we shall never know what caused many of these fires, it is surprising in going over reports how many fires could have been prevented if someone had just stopped to think and taken a precaution or two. Let us note just a few items:

	No. of Fires	Loss
Chimneys, flues—defective or overheated	67,500	$40,000,000.00
Sparks on roofs	42,500	10,400,000.00
Defective or overheated heating equipment	49,000	24,500,000.00

Rubbish	18,000	1,400,000.00
Electrical, fixed services; fire due to misuse, or faulty wiring and equipment	53,500	33,500,000.00
Electrical power consuming appliances	17,000	7,000,000.00
Lamps, lanterns, and stoves	19,000	5,200,000.00
Spontaneous ignition	13,000	16,600,000.00
Sparks from machinery, friction	3,800	3,300,000.00
Churches	2,600	4,500,000.00
Amusement halls	2,900	4,700,000.00

Bishop, there isn't anything that worries us more in our Church in our fear of fires than poor wiring and rubbish. In this picture it shows very distinctly how a couple of live wires coming together can cause a spark that starts a big blaze. Sometimes as we go around the Church and see the piles of rubbish, crepe paper, etc., our hearts almost stand still. Sometimes because of neglect our little children sit on a "keg of dynamite" as far as their little lives are concerned because of some of our carelessness.

Some time ago we visited a little Church where, way up in the attic, accessible only by a winding, wooden stair, was a classroom. One of the legs of the stove, the only means of heat, had been broken off, and a loose brick took the place of this particular leg. Boys in a scuffle could knock out this brick. Only one thing would follow. It would tip over the stove, and those boys and girls could die like rats.

We haven't said very much in this little reminder of fire hazards about the endangering of lives. Bishop, "a stitch in time saves nine." Just a little precaution will make our sleep at night more wholesome. Spontaneous combustion is like a thief in the night. You can't tell when it will happen. It generally is caused by an oily rag, or it even comes from wet coal stored away. One of our biggest meetinghouses in Salt Lake City came within an ace of burning to the ground because of wet coal in storage exposed to wood.

So that you will not think this note too pessimistic, let me say that the insurance companies can't understand why our losses are so few. It is because of eternal vigilance. Remember, bishop, we are carrying our own insurance. Let's save the Church money, but let it never be said of us that a life was lost because we failed to take care of some detail.

STORY SIXTY-FOUR

BISHOP, ARE YOU TIGHT?

As with the *priest,* so with the *people.* In your ward financial program this is doubly true. Your people won't expect you to do more than your ability will warrant, but they will expect you to be just as game as you expect them to be. If you have a big padlock on your purse and a bull dog doing a sentinel job over your money bag, you will find this particular disease is contagious. It is one thing to be frugal—it is entirely a different thing to squeeze the eagles on your dollars and expect others of the same financial status as yourself to build up the local treasury.

In my experience in going from ward to ward I have found some of the most miserable failures in money raising because the bishop didn't take the lead. I have in mind a ward whose chapel and other buildings were deplorable, simply a disgrace to the Church and an embarrassment as strangers would pass through, yet the people of that ward were in good financial circumstances and as a whole could raise a good-sized lump without hurting anyone. This particular bishop had "a thousand cattle on a thousand hills," and yet he wouldn't budge. He had raised his family, he was near seventy, and yet he didn't want his pocketbook materially disturbed. Of course, his people didn't come through. I said to him, "Bishop, put your name at the head of the list and make it a thousand." In my judgment that attitude was the main thing needed to put that ward right up there where the live ones swim. Bishop, you can't take those sheep with you—neither can you take your lands and your money.

By the way, in attending a meeting recently where a ward was trying to raise funds for a chapel, I was really surprised to get this observation from a member of the committee: "Bishop, we are having the hardest time with some of our financially independent old folks." You'd think those most responsive to a call for a new chapel, those who could see their closing days more than well financed, would part with some of their money with the least resistance. Sometimes I wonder if at times the youth, as it were, in the middle of raising and educating their children, in the most expensive time of their lives, are not making greater sacrifices than some of our older folks whose days of financial worries are over.

Bishop, set the example, and they will follow. You can't pass the buck.

> "Jock, will ye dine wi' me th' morn's nicht?"
> "Ay, I will."
> "Grand,—eight o'clock at yer hoose."

The most moth-eaten story of all Scotch stories:

> When a Scotchman opened his purse three moths flew out.

Bishop, don't be Scotch.

STORY SIXTY-FIVE

BISHOP, AVOID ACCIDENTS?

The accompanying picture tells a story, but it isn't fiction. It happens every day in every city. Deaths as a result of the neglect of attention to little things would fill several good-sized cemeteries. Bishop, it seems there are some accidents that are unavoidable, but most of them could be avoided if we were more careful. A trench is left open, and a leg or neck is broken; a board with a nail sticking up vertically is left in a well traveled path, causing lockjaw and maybe the death of a boy who comes that way at night; a metal bucket is left on a roof; a wind comes up; the bucket is dropped on an innocent passer-by and five children are left motherless.

Yes, these are only little bits of things, but they bring the heart throbs in our lives. Now look at this unfortunate fellow coming involuntarily down those steps. It isn't the custodian—it is a stranger to the Church premises who was coming to a scheduled meeting. He has been hunting for the place of meeting. He thinks this particular door opens into that particular committee room. Because he doesn't know the local geography of that chapel, he steps into a death trap. We are not exaggerating: If this poor fellow hits those steps just right, either contacting his backbone or his head, he is likely to be an invalid for life or a dead man. He thought he was coming into a well-lighted room, but he has dropped into a dark abyss, and if he loses his hold on that doorknock, he's a goner. Now, bishop, this accident could have been avoided. If that door had to be there, then guards of some kind should have been just inside the door. "Danger" in big letters should have been written on the inside approach to that door.

Bishop, I was in a Church building just the other day and I found a hazard exactly like the illustration here. Why don't we consider life more precious than we do? Instead of saying often as an unfortunate victim of someone's carelessness is put under six feet of ground "It's too bad," we should say "It should have been otherwise."

A few weeks ago I called at a farmhouse. Less than fifty feet from the back door within the shade of three or four lovely playing kids was a hole four feet wide, going straight down fifty feet to a valve or shutoff. That open gap in mother earth had been there for at least months. When my eyes hit that yawning death trap, as kinky as my hair is, it stood up straight. I ask myself this question time and time again as I see such sights—why are we so careless, why do we put on the Lord the responsibilities we do—of putting his arms around the innocent folks subjected to such dynamite? Yes, some of these examples of carelessness might just as well be sticks of dynamite right under our shoes.

Bishop, let's avoid accidents in and about our Church buildings. Let's avoid such epitaphs as these:

Here lie the bones of Mary Green;
She washed her clothes in gasoline.

Here he lies—to cry, it was too late;
But this is how he met his fate:
He entered a door with a ten foot drop,
No warning there he was to stop.

STORY SIXTY-SIX

BISHOP, WHICH CUSTODIAN IS YOURS?

As with the custodian, so with the Church! Will you please study this picture with me just for a second or two? You can tell at a glance what your Church will look like in a month or two if that tramp of a fellow "rules the roost" on your Church premises. No matter how well it looked when the keys were turned over to him, it will look like a pigpen just as soon as the spiders have had a chance to weave their webs, and the flies have had time to have a few loafing parties. That second fellow is an archenemy of cleanliness and a friend to fire and accident hazards. He is the eternal foe of sanctity and order and the best invitation in the world for disorder and irreverence to walk into your Church and put their feet on the desk.

That other fellow, neat and tidy, breathes the first law of heaven, "order and obedience." His very attiude, without the hint of a command, suggests cleanliness next to godliness, and "this is a holy place."

With the fellow on the left you face broken windows, tumble-down fences, and the cows destroying the Church landscape. In the hands of the other fellow, culture and refinement will be sustained, and you will have a place maintained that will be your pride and a place where you are happy to bring your friends or the stranger within your gates. In the hands of the first caretaker, (if we may so misuse the English language) you will show extravagance and waste and a building in twenty years, if he should stay that long, depreciated to nothing. If that smiling fellow holding that healthy pushbroom, standing in front of well-kept lawn and garden, has your Church twenty years, that building will be worth more when the twenty years are up than when he took over.

The first man is expensive and crude. The second man is economic and suggests worship and the finer things of life.

Bishop, did you hire that fellow to be your custodian because he was on relief? If that's the only reason, get rid of him quickly. Your philosophy is bad, and in the long run you're heaping on to your people a shameful liability.

Bishop, pick your man, and, yes, we'll go one further: Ask the Lord to help you get the proper man for this important responsibility in your ward. Pay your man well and get a man old and young love to mingle with. It's the best money you spend.

STORY SIXTY-SEVEN

BISHOP, DO YOU PREACH DOLLARS TOO MUCH?

It goes without saying that you can't run your ward without money, but do you cheapen the pulpit by an everlasting harangue for money? Bishop, in plain Anglo-Saxon, you'll kill influence as a bishop and defeat the very purpose of your ecclesiastical setup if you persist in making of the sacredness of your chapel a collection agency. Your chapel is a sanctuary. Its primary purpose is to preach the gospel of Jesus Christ. Your good people come to Church to be spiritually fed, not to be reminded continually of the budget deficit and that your building fund is dragging its heels. Your people must be reminded of those obligations, and no one of your flock can consistently presume to be a real member of the Church and not carry his part of the financial burden. But, bishop, organize yourself, and plan your procedure so that money is collected in a quiet, systematic way. Appoint your committees so they function away from that sacred place, the chapel. Big things in life are done quietly. A bishop who is wise will delegate this money collecting for Church purposes, largely, if not entirely, to others. When he does this, he makes others happy in being honored with such responsibility and leaves himself free to do those things that come more particularly in the category of the things he should do to be a real father of the ward. Again may we repeat, nothing marks you as a leader more than to delegate authority.

Things are serious with you, bishop, if when you arise in the pulpit, it is a fifty-fifty bet that your congregation is going to get a financial "blessing." If you want to make yourself unpopular and kill your influence, just foreverlastingly *spank* your members from the pulpit about their dollars and cents Church obligations. Your pleas, instead of being conducive or good, are going to bounce back at you and tend to flatten the best-made money plans.

In all your rush to fill your bishop destiny, don't forget what it is all about. Let's eternally keep ourselves definitely on the beam. Let us keep before us the mariner's chart and hold the wheel accordingly. Let's stay on the course. When we overdo things, sometimes it takes a lash and the overturning of the money changers' tables.

Bishop, let's keep our chapels hallowed places when we go to worship. Let's keep them a haven where we get solace from a storm-tossed sea. In this spot we get comfort; in this place the heavens are opened to our understanding. Here we assemble to receive healing balm that helps us in our loss of loved ones and the struggle of life.

Bishop, don't let this little sketch mean you. No more do we want our places polluted with the noise of silver any more than the Savior of mankind wanted the sacred halls of his temple to echo with bellowing of cattle or the bleating of sheep.

STORY SIXTY-EIGHT

HAWAIIAN FISHING

In this picture you see a Hawaiian on the top of a mountain overlooking the ocean. He stands there going through motions that remind you of a Boy Scout in his signaling stunts. Yes, that's exactly what this native is doing. He is signaling to his fellows who stand there with their nets a half mile away, following his instructions as to where to fish.

In Hawaii the water of the ocean is as clear as crystal. You can see the bottom though it's hundreds of feet below. By standing on that lookout spot, while a long distance from his fellow fisherman, by the shadows and the light this fellow can tell where the fish are running. When they throw their nets, by his guidance, their reward will be a hundred baskets. Otherwise they would wear themselves out meandering about in the rocks snagging an occasional fish. By this proper viewpoint their fishing is made expert. The natives have come from miles around to fill their baskets because of right guidance.

May I repeat, do we mortals here below get far enough away from ourselves really to, with some accuracy and viewpoint, see ourselves pass by? Yes, do we tramp around in the mud and rocks of our lives catching, as it were, just an occasional fish?

How we could help one another if we'd get on the top of the mountain overlooking our activities and from a distance see the lights and shadows. We'd all rejoice, and our reward would be basketfuls.

"Where there is no vision, the people perish."

STORY SIXTY-NINE

CONSTANT AIM

Many men in life fail because their aim is not constant. "Hitch your wagon to a star" and you are bound to get somewhere. But be "dead sure" your aim is definite and fixed. Settle down to one thing and give it all the gunpowder you possess, and you are bound to win blue ribbons.

Now this fellow in the cartoon, as far as ploughing this field is concerned, is not getting anywhere. The fact of the matter is he's going in circles. Here's the story as I heard it:

It is a story of an immigrant from the old country. He had worked in a factory all his life and didn't know any more about farming than a farmer knows about making watches. But while everything was new in this strange world he had just entered, there had to be a day of beginning no matter how many awkward moves were to be made. Well, his first job was ploughing. He got back of the team, but before saying "git up" to those sturdy horses the first question to come from the new ploughman was naturally, "Mr. Brown, now how shall I keep these furrows straight?"

The farmer's instructions were as follows, "John, do you see that black spot up there at the end of the field? Now you just keep your eye on that and your ploughing will be straight."

Now John did that very thing. He kept his eyes on that black thing.

About two hours later imagine Mr. Brown's surprise. He was confronted by his new farm hand. The horses were all in a lather, and the fellow who held the plough was about "fagged out." John yelled at the top of his voice to the owner of the farm, "Mr. Brown, could you get me another pig. This one I've been following is all in."

Yes, the newcomer was working his head off, but his plough was changing its course every minute.

STORY SEVENTY

WE PLAY OUR GREATEST TUNES IN TIME OF STORM

An old fable tells us of a king who had the ambition to build the greatest musical instrument in the world. To carry out his plan he built a huge castle and strung the wires from tower to tower.

They say the only time the big violin thrilled the world was in time of storm. It played its greatest tunes when the walls of the castle were beaten with the tempest.

"It is a characteristic of small men to avoid emergencies—of great men to meet them."

Someone else has said, "When trouble comes, wise men take to their work—weak men take to the woods."

In many spots of this world trees are so thick and close together that it really doesn't make much difference whether each tree sends its roots deep into the soil or not. They stand because of those about them. What is really important in life is that each of us get hold of the firm ground and like the oak in the lonely place, stand on our own feet.

This man Harry Emerson Fosdick has been a great stimulus to America and for that matter to the world. Great souls like his stand like a big pine of the forest encouraging those about him to be their best and fill the measure of their existence. *A Great Time to be Alive* was a shot in the arm to a world stupefied after World War No. II. Now is the time for the world to meet the challenges head-on. Let's play our greatest tunes in time of storm.

Winston Churchill, bless his soul, no matter what political disappointments he may have had and whether or not his generation fully appreciates him—his footprints will stand out in the history of mankind like the tracks of a giant dinosaur. In time of storm he gave to the world rhythm that stirred the souls of half the population of the world. His war cry, "Sweat, blood, and tears," will echo through the ages.

In the American Museum of Art in New York the original painting of "Washington Crossing the Delaware" glued my feet to the floor. Without challenges like that Christmas evening on that floating ice, and Valley Forge, you wouldn't have had a George Washington. Without a Gettsyburg you wouldn't have had a Lincoln. Without a persecuted people driven together by adversity you wouldn't have had a Brigham Young. It took those days that "tried men's souls" to develop that leadership that, too, will be heard through the ages. As Fosdick puts it, "Some eras are like a lullaby—some are like a spur. Which of the two is likely in the end to be the greater?"

The important thing is, can we take it on the chin? What does adversity do to us? Does it floor us or does it bring out the gold that God has planted in us?

"If thou faint in the day of adversity, thy strength is small."

Let me tell you a corn story:

About three years ago it was my pleasure to call on the mayor of Nauvoo, Illinois, in his place of business. Because of its unusual quality and size, two baskets of corn there caught my eye. Of course I inquired about it. "That is that hybrid corn you have been reading about," said the mayor.

"How many bushels to the acre?" I asked.

"Eighty to eighty-five," was his answer.

"How many bushels to the acre of the ordinary corn?" was my next question.

"Forty to fifty," was his response.

I had been reading about this improved grain, and my interest was doubly keen. Corn is a big item in these United States of America. Hogs and corn, and corn and hogs. I did a little figuring myself one day, and if I was at all in keeping with good arithmetic, there is enough corn raised in the United States each year, if all the cobs of corn were placed end to end, there would be enough corn to make a roadbed over a hundred feet wide encompassing the entire globe, including the ocean spaces. Now that makes us all interested in Indian corn whether we are partial to ham or our most favorite breakfast cereal, corn flakes.

Here are a few of the high spots of one of the stories in the development of hybrid corn as I remember them:

A little fellow by the name of Pheister awakened one morning with the notion that he could give America a better grade of corn. He read all he could about corn, got all the tips he could from the agricultural department and then went ahead. (We'll cut through the lot, so to speak, and make the story short.) He knew one of the first things he had to do was to control the pollination of the corn flower. In other words, the pollination just couldn't be promiscuous. He himself, Mr. Pheister, would say which plants would carry on wedlock and, if so, with whom. I suppose this is what they call selective breeding.

Well, when the corn he had planted came to the tassel or flower stage, the hero of our story tied a paper sack, if you please, around each corn blossom. Of course he would be ridiculed—he expected it. In fact the people as they drove by in their cars tapped their heads as per courtesy extended Columbus when he said the earth is round.

Over a period of about five years he'd planted, selected, and harvested. He had determined to give the world a better ear of corn, but it cost him all his accumulated finances and had pretty nearly ruined his health. All he had to show for his toil and worry thus far was a small bag of kernels of grain. It would take one more season to finish his program of experimentation. Could he go that much further? He pulled himself together and planted again. All he had in the world was now in the ground.

In a few months the small experimental garden looked well. But the drought came. The corn cried for a drink of water, but rain did not come. Pheister's neighbors who before had scoffed at his plans now pitied him. Said they, "Pheister, why don't you get some barrels of water and save that corn? All you have in the world is there."

Pheister straightened up and looked his friends in the eye and defiantly cried back, "I put water on nothing. That corn is going to take it on the chin."

By the time rain finally came, one-third of the corn had dried up. What life remained in the corn crop started again to assert itself. But it got another punch in the eye. From over the western skies came clouds of grasshoppers. Thousands pounced down on what was left of the experimental farm. Again the neighbors observed with sympathy Pheister's losses. Said they, "Pheister, why don't you get some netting and tie around those few remaining live plants?"

Again our friend faced his farm folk. "That corn is going to take it on the chin."

Well, the grasshoppers, after they had feasted and ruined, finally picked up baggage and left. Just a handful of plants remained. But when Pheister harvested, while he had only a handful, he had a corn to give to America that was a "*Thoroughbred.*" It could take it on the chin. It could take the attacks of the grasshoppers. It could stand the fire of the drought.

Eighty-five bushels to the acre!

Are we hybrid pieces of humanity? Are we thoroughbreds? Can we take life's droughts? Can we take the "grasshoppers?"

INDEX

CONTENTS—*Continued*

INDEX—*Continued*